READING
RUTH

READING RUTH

*Birth, Redemption,
and the Way of Israel*

**LEON KASS
HANNAH MANDELBAUM**

PAUL DRY BOOKS
Philadelphia 2021

First Paul Dry Books Edition, 2021

Paul Dry Books, Inc.
Philadelphia, Pennsylvania
www.pauldrybooks.com

Printed in the United States of America

Library of Congress Control Number: 2020951613

ISBN-13: 978-1-58988-158-7

IN MEMORY OF

Amy Apfel Kass

אשת חיל

Contents

Preface

This little volume offers a reading—an *interpretation*—of the Book of Ruth, one of the most beloved books of the Hebrew Bible. It also seeks to recreate the *experience* of reading Ruth—an activity—as we, the authors, underwent it together. We hope that our commentary will bring the story to life, shed light on its place in the biblical canon, reveal some of its teachings and wisdom, and, last but hardly least, display a way of engaging the text that makes such insights possible.

We did not start out intending to write a book. We began, in the Fall of 2015, merely seeking to give comfort to each other following the death of our beloved Amy Apfel Kass—wife of 54 years to Leon; grandmother ("Gaga") of 16 years to Hannah. Leon was living, then as now, in Washington, DC; Hannah was living, then as now, in Jerusalem. The idea was Hannah's, suggested in one of her daily calls: "Zaydeh (Yiddish for "Grandpa")," she said, "perhaps you would like to read something with me." Leon grabbed the offer: a log brought to a drowning man. We settled easily and quickly on the Book of Ruth. Not only was it short and lovely. It also had special meaning for Leon. Some twenty years earlier, Amy and he had made a discovery in the Book of Ruth that they thought might be the key to understanding its meaning, and they had spoken about working on it in the future. But that future never arrived, and Leon had forgotten the insight. He was therefore particularly keen to see whether, with Hannah's help, it could be recovered.

From mid-October until the end of December 2015, we spent an hour on Face Time two or three days a week, reading Ruth aloud line by line—Hannah in Hebrew, both of us in English—discussing at most two or three verses a session. The sentence read out, we asked each other what was going on—with the characters, with the plot, with the thought of the story. Already in the first or second session, Hannah made a critical observation that promptly brought back the forgotten insight of her grandparents. (We will point it out when we get there.) Leon started taking notes on what was being said as the ongoing close reading brought us new observations and insights, as well as new questions and perplexities. We began to notice the prevalence of certain words, themes, and emphases. We followed up hints that led us to examine other biblical texts that seemed relevant. Our appreciation of the story increased, as did our love for its characters and our sense of its significance. Initial differences of opinion were hashed out, often leading to mutual understandings different from the ones with which each of us had begun. By the end, we decided to write up our notes, to see what if anything they amounted to.

Leon was the first draftsman, Hannah the first critical reviewer. The process led to additional discoveries and additional questions. New drafts led to new critiques, leading again to new insights and more questions. Life, alas, intervened. Hannah entered the Israeli Air Force for her national service, leaving little time for sustained work. Haphazardly over the next two years, we looked at other sources that came to our attention, sometimes suggested by friends who knew of our activity: an essay on Ruth by Cynthia Ozick and another on Naomi by Maurice Samuel; the traditional commentary on the Book of Ruth, *Ruth Rabbah*; an online essay by Alan Rubenstein on the love of Ruth and Boaz; and, very late in the process, Yael Ziegler's marvelous book, *Ruth: From Alienation to Monarchy*.

Although continuing to emphasize our own experiential reading of Ruth, our later drafts would add—mainly as Notes—gleanings from these sources, either to embellish or to challenge our own interpretations. The current version also includes small additions, again to the Notes, prompted by comments from friends who read late drafts in the summer of 2020 and from three seminar discussions of Ruth that Leon and Alan Rubenstein led in July 2020 for the Tikvah Fund's Online Open University. Further incubation and reading more secondary sources would, no doubt, enrich our understanding. But since we are mainly interested in demonstrating what can be learned from dwelling immediately and intimately with the plain text itself, we have put an end to reading and revising and gladly send forth our work to readers unknown.

In doing so, we have been forced—admittedly late in the process, and by our editor and publisher—to imagine our ideal reader. Truth to tell, we imagine her or him to be somewhat like ourselves: whether young or old a lover of stories with a taste for character and artistry; a serious but open-minded seeker of wisdom regarding enduring human concerns; a friend (or potential friend) of the Hebrew Bible, receptive to its beauty and open to its teachings. We assume no prior religious commitments, biblical scholarship, or previous knowledge of this text. We require only a willingness to suspend disbelief, to enter the story with a sympathetic imagination, and to slow down and read carefully with us, hoping to discover thereby something humanly important that you, our ideal reader, had not known before.

We are aware—not least because some of them have told us—that many people do not believe that the Book of Ruth has anything much to teach us. It is, they point out, "only" a beautiful story, a lovely and entertaining work of art, not a philosophical treatise, codebook of legal commandments, or handbook of moral maxims. Moreover, it was written ages ago about a world no longer ours. All true enough, but not persuasive. In the Hebrew Bible—and right from the story of Creation—stories are the main vehicle of instruction. They teach not didactically but indirectly and through example, by allowing us to re-experience our life and our world in the mirror of a well-crafted tale. Like all great stories, the biblical stories move us precisely because they continue to speak powerfully to certain permanent human questions: our place in the world and how to live in it; the meaning of love and death, man and woman, parent and child, friend and enemy; the nature of good and evil, truth and falsehood, justice and injustice; our relation to the divine. Engaging both the head and the heart, the biblical stories, like all great stories, help build character by furnishing the imagination, sharpening the mind's eye, and educating our moral and aesthetic sensibilities—all without telling us that they are doing so.

Many of us love to tell stories, and most of us love to hear them. But to hear and read, and to study and discuss, the best stories told by the best storytellers is more than a way of passing time. It is a way of deepening time, by taking us to the profoundly humanizing truths contained in the ordinary surfaces of our experience. With the help of a great storyteller, we can see in and through the commonplace the things that really matter. To be sure, stories are entertaining, but at their best they inform and re-form us by dramatizing belief and rendering feeling thoughtful. All this has been our experience of reading and living with the story of Ruth.

We are constrained to say something also about how we read and how we interpret what we have read. Amateur—non-scholarly—readers that we are, we have not consciously adopted any "method" worthy of the name. Because this commentary displays openly our way of reading, we advise our readers to experience it for themselves as they join us in reading Ruth. The proof of the reading lies in what we—and you—will get out of it.

Still, we can say a few things by way of anticipation. As already noted, we read slowly; indeed, very slowly. We think every word matters. We attend to linguistic clues, echoes, and juxtapositions. Equally important, we attend to silences and to the things that are not said. Most important, we try to imagine ourselves present on the scene, inhabiting in sequence the persons of the drama, speaking their speeches, hearing the others speak, imagining the unspoken reactions to the things said. As does the text, we pay special attention to the living conversations, as the characters disclose themselves to each other—and to us. The text being elliptical, we accept its invitation to speculate where there are silences and ambiguities in the account. We offer and consider competing hypotheses and explanations, often leaving the matter undecided. We are happy to acknowledge the mysterious, the ineffable, and even what may be providential in human affairs—not least because we have experienced them in reading Ruth together.

Our chief goal has been to make the text come alive to us—and now, also to you. We have wanted less to learn *about* it, more to experience and to live *with* it. We have taken pains to let it show us what it is about and what it hopes to teach us, and to learn from the book how it wishes to be read. Stepping back from the text, we have also explored its themes and questions, hoping to glean its insights about those enduring human concerns. Finally, in writing up our experience of reading and conversing, we have sought not only to illustrate how we have read but also to display how this reading has affected us the readers—from across the generations and between our own.*

About the Text

Translation and Transliteration: In studying Ruth, we have mainly used a bilingual edition, available online (http://www.mechon-mamre.org/p/pt/pt0.htm), compris-

---

* For the authors' personal afterthoughts, see page 111.

ing the Masoretic Hebrew text and the 1917 Jewish Publication Society English translation. A complete English translation of Ruth, presented sequentially as excerpts throughout this book, is largely taken from that source, but modified here and there according to our own sense of what seems most fitting. We have sought the most literal translation compatible with readable English.

Transliterations of Hebrew words largely follow the rules of Encyclopedia Judaica, 2nd edition. Therefore, aspirated ב and פ are rendered *v* and *f*, respectively; aspirated כ is indicated by *kh*, and aspirated ג and ד forms are rendered as *g* and *d* respectively. However, aspirated ת is indicated as *th*. We deviate from the Encyclopedia Judaica rules in avoiding diacritical markings: therefore ח is rendered *ch*, and צ is rendered *ts*. Furthermore, א and ע are both indicated with an apostrophe (' and ', respectively) when they appear in the first position in a syllable. Final unvoiced ה is indicated by *h* at the end of the word. Furthermore, ק is rendered *q*, not *k*. As in the Encyclopedia Judaica system, the *dagesh forte* is indicated by a doubled consonant, except when it appears on the letters *shin* or *tsade*, in which cases it is not indicated. Silent *yod* (as in צאינה) is not indicated.

Citations from Ruth will be given numerically, chapter and verse. Citations from other biblical sources will first identify the book.

The Notes: To improve the reader's experience of the printed page, nearly all notes—including many (often lengthy) comments that extend or qualify what is in the text—have been placed in the Notes section at the back of the book. All citations and attributions appear there as well. In a few instances, especially relevant substantive material that might have gone to the Notes we have included in the text where it seemed that its enrichment of the discussion was worth disturbing the narrative flow.

Readers may observe that the style of the Notes is less dialectical and playful than the style of the main text. This should not be interpreted as implying that the Notes are the more serious business. On the contrary, the stylistic difference highlights a primary purpose of this book: to display the lived and lively experience of Reading Ruth.

READING
RUTH

Everyone loves the Book of Ruth. It's easy to see why. The book's three main characters are admirable: Ruth is a loyal and devoted daughter-in-law and a paragon of friendship, grace, and delicacy; her mother-in-law Naomi is a resilient and resourceful woman, wholly and wisely devoted to Ruth's well-being; Boaz is a noble and gracious gentleman, worthy of Ruth and a model of rectitude. If you like stories of female solidarity, or celebrations of strong women, you have here an example of both, in spades: the robust friendship of Ruth and Naomi, unique among biblical women, is a paradigm of mutual regard and devotion. If you prefer love stories, you will be equally pleased: though not a torrid tale of passionate romance, the Book of Ruth recounts a slowly emerging yet deep and durable bond between two virtuous soul mates. If yours is a taste for happy endings, this story moves from famine and exile to homecoming and harvest, from death and sterility to fertility and birth, from isolation and grief to joy and union, from sin and corruption to return and redemption. Finally, readers partial to tales about reversals of fortune, or the transcendence of cultural barriers, will delight in this account of how a woman from a despised nation becomes the ancestress of Israelite royalty.

What's not to like?

Yet, given its honored place in the Hebrew Bible, surely the Book of Ruth must be more than a Cinderella story, a woman's rise from rags to riches, from misery to glory. What, we wonder, is it doing in the biblical canon, and what is it trying to teach? Even more simply, what is this book *really* about?

Reading Ruth in search of its wisdom, we have been struck by the presence of many important matters. First, despite being a decidedly personal story, its outermost frame is political: the book opens with reference to an earlier era in Israelite history, the troubled Age of Judges (recounted in the biblical Book of Judges), and finishes with an allusion to the coming Age of Kings (as recounted in the Books of Samuel and Kings)—and ultimately, according to later Jewish tradition, to the redemptive arrival of the messiah. The fate of Ruth (and Naomi) is thus linked to the fate of the nation. Second, the story touches on the relationship between Israel and its neighbors—indeed, between Israel and its archenemy Moab—largely through the delicate subjects of intermarriage, assimilation of foreigners into an established culture, and (perhaps) religious "conversion." Third, uniquely in the Bible, the Book of Ruth explores together the subjects of friendship and of marital love. Although it is famously a story about (female) friendship, it features more prominently a concern for marriage and the redemptive possibility of procreation: the central and unifying theme of the entire book. Fourth, this concern for birth and lineage is connected to concern for land and its inheritance; release from barrenness goes hand-in-hand with recovery of lost land, keeping the land in possession of families, and keeping families rooted in the land. In this same context, fifth, we learn the importance of being one's brother's keeper: levirate (or protective) marriage, as legislated in the Hebrew Bible (Deuteronomy 25:5–10), keeps childless people from disappearing without a trace and from breaking the continuity among the generations. Sixth, just below the surface, the story contains a radically hopeful teaching about redemption from the stains of historical iniquity, as descendants of long-ago incestuous abominations become the ancestors of the Lord's anointed. Finally, suffused through the entire story is the virtue of *chesed* ("loyal devotion" or "gracious kindness"), human and divine, revealing its saving power in human affairs.*

We will explore these themes and their significance as they emerge from a close reading of this brief, entrancing, and disarmingly simple fairy tale of a story.

Title and Overview

Our book is known in the Jewish tradition as *Megillath Ruth*, the Scroll of Ruth. Its author is not identified; neither is the time of its composition. We are not told why the book is named for Ruth rather than, say, for her mother-in-law Naomi. We do know, however, that it is one of only two biblical books—the other is Esther—named for a woman. It is also the *only* biblical book named for a foreign figure, and Ruth's foreign-

---

Chesed, transliterating חסד, is a disyllabic word, *che-sed*, accented on the first syllable. The initial sound is a guttural version of "heh," nothing like the opening sound of "cheese" or "chair."

ness is repeatedly emphasized. Putting these two facts together, we might expect to find in Ruth an exploration of the unique conjunction of "the woman question" and "the outsider question." If we read carefully, we will not be disappointed.

The Book of Ruth comprises four chapters, a mere eighty-five verses in all (22, 23, 18, and 22 verses, respectively). Despite this remarkable brevity, the book's settings and tone vary greatly, proceeding from a sorrowful journey to the kingdom of Moab and back; to a gracious encounter in the fields of barley; to an intimate engagement on the threshing floor; to an inspiring gathering at the city gate followed by a celebrated birth.

In the first chapter, the action begins with the Israelite man Elimelech who, to escape a famine in the land, takes his wife Naomi and their two sons from Bethlehem into the neighboring land of Moab. Ten years later, all three men have died and Naomi, accompanied by her Moabite daughter-in-law Ruth, leads a grief-stricken return to Bethlehem. At the heart of this chapter is a conversation that features Ruth's great speech of devotion to Naomi.

In the second chapter, initiative resides with Ruth, who goes to glean subsistence for herself and Naomi in the field of Boaz, a distinguished and prosperous landowner. At the heart of this chapter is the noontime conversation between Boaz and Ruth, initiated by Boaz.

In the third chapter Naomi launches the action, sending Ruth to the threshing floor after the last day of winnowing to seduce Boaz into marriage. At the heart of this chapter is the midnight conversation between Ruth and Boaz, with Ruth now in the lead.

In the final chapter, which occurs the next day at the city gate, Boaz seizes the initiative in order to gain Ruth as his wife. At the heart of this chapter is the negotiation through which Boaz acquires from a rival kinsman the right to marry Ruth. Later the city rejoices when a child is born to Ruth and Boaz: a child who becomes the forerunner of the Davidic line.

Suitably oriented, we are ready to start reading. Our headings will reflect the story's thematic divisions, or what one might call the drama's sequential Acts and Scenes; these do not always coincide with the chapter divisions that, here as elsewhere in the Hebrew Bible, were not part of the original text but were later introduced by medieval Christian scholars.

Dark Beginnings: Famine, Removal, and Death

Our story begins by reporting a single Israelite family's flight from famine into a neighboring land, a move that will be followed by a rapid descent into misery and desolation. (Unless otherwise noted, all citations are to the Book of Ruth, chapter and verse.)

> And it happened (*vayehi*) in the days of the judging of judges (*shefot hashoftim*), that there happened (*vayehi*) a famine in the land. And there went a [certain] man (*'ish*) of Bethlehem in Judah to sojourn (*lagur*) in the fields of Moab (*sedei Mo'av*)—he, and his wife, and his two sons. And the name of the man was Elimelech, and the name of his wife Naomi, and the name of his two sons Mahlon and

Chilion, Ephrathites of Bethlehem in Judah. And
they came into the fields of Moab, and remained
there [literally, "they were there"; *vayyiheyu
sham*]. (1:1–2)

The account opens prosaically, telling us when, where,
who, what, and (apparently) why: the bare facts setting
the stage for a story. Perhaps we should simply take them
at face value and read on. But interesting things emerge
if we look more closely.

The story begins in the Promised Land during the
time when the Children of Israel were ruled by judges,
before the coming of the monarchy. (The story will end
by giving the genealogy of David, the glorious second
king of Israel, whose name is the book's final word.) The
judges ruled for three hundred years, from about 1400
BCE to about 1100 BCE. We do not know when during
this period our story takes place, but whatever the exact
date, it was not a peaceful and healthy time. The (dou-
ble) use of the expression, "it happened" (*vayehi*), seems
to prefigure trouble and misfortune—a point under-
lined by a rabbinic play on words that suggests understanding *vayehi* as two separate nouns: *vay*, "woe," and
hi, "lamentation."

The first trouble appears immediately: a famine in
the land. Why a famine? We are not told, so perhaps it
does not matter. But readers of the Bible, aware of God's
prior threats to inflict agricultural failure as punishment
for national sinfulness, will be tempted to seek an explanation in such misconduct, especially when it takes the
form of idolatry.

The Book of Judges does report that in the period

after the death of Joshua, when a series of judges ruled, idolatry was a recurrent problem; yet famine was not among the punishments the Lord meted out to His wayward people, and the word "famine," *ra'av*, does not occur in the Book of Judges. In our text, a possible clue may reside in the odd expression, "days of the judging of the judges"—instead of "days of the judges." Was this merely a lawless period of widespread evildoing and disputes among the tribes, requiring abundant judicial activity? (The Book of Judges twice proclaims the defining fact of anarchy: "In those days there was no king in Israel; each man did whatever was right in his own eyes" [Judges 17:6 and 21:25, the last sentence of the whole book].) Or were these also times of corrupt *judges*, whose own crimes were greater than the crimes they adjudicated and upon which a (divine) punishment—the "judging *of* the judges"—was rendered in the form of famine?

In either case, these were doubly bad times in the Promised Land: bad deeds, no food. What were people to do?

Most people, it seems, stayed put and waited out the famine. But a certain man—an *'ish*, a man of standing—decided to leave the country. Why should we be interested in him, and what, we wonder, are we to make of his singularity? Should we regard him as a maverick and outlier in Israel, or as a paradigm of Israelite initiative and enterprise—or, alternatively, of Israelite waywardness? The man came from the town of Bethlehem (ironically, "house of bread") in the territory of the tribe of Judah, the leading and most political tribe. Readers familiar with Genesis will suspect that the man's tribal

origin may be significant. For we remember that the
eponymous founder of the tribe of Judah also quit his
own community in a time of trouble, after his brother
Joseph was sold into Egypt:

> And it happened (*vayehi*) at that time that Judah
> went down from his brethren, and turned in (*vayyet*)
> to a certain Adullamite (*'ish 'adullami*), whose name
> was Hirah. (Genesis 38:1)

Again *vayehi*, "it happened": more trouble afoot. Judah's
temporary but disastrous sojourn with Hirah (later
called "his *friend* Hirah the Adullamite") includes the
infamous episode of his encounter with his daughter-in-
law Tamar. It also contains three other significant links
to our present tale: the first mention of friendship in
the Bible and the first of only three biblical friendships
(along with those of Ruth and Naomi, and David and
Jonathan); the first biblical instance of the levirate duty
to raise up children to brothers who have died childless; and, at the end, the (incestuous) birth of Perez—
son of Judah by Tamar—who (we will learn soon) is the
ancestor of Boaz, the male lead and heroic performer of
the levirate (or, better, levirate-*like*) duty in our Book
of Ruth.

Because we will often refer to it, let's quickly sum-
marize the story of Judah among the Adullamites. Judah
marries a Canaanite woman, has three sons by her, and
takes for Er, his eldest son, a Canaanite wife named
Tamar. When Er is slain by the Lord for his wickedness, Judah instructs his second son Onan to perform
the levirate duty with Tamar, to raise up children to his

dead brother. But it happens (*vayehi*) that Onan, realizing that the offspring will not be his, takes his pleasure of the woman but, rather than fulfilling his duty, spills his seed on the ground; for this wickedness the Lord slays him also. Judah promises Tamar he will bring her his youngest son Shelah when he is grown. But Judah reneges on this promise, fearing that he might be bereaved a third time. Taking matters into her own hands, Tamar dresses up as a harlot and places herself in her father-in-law's path as he comes from the sheep shearing. Not recognizing who she is, Judah, newly a widower, turns in (*vayyet*) to lie with her and she becomes pregnant. When accused of playing the harlot, she exposes Judah as the father, and he is in turn compelled to acknowledge that "she is more righteous than I." Tamar gives birth to twins, Zerah and Perez. In the immediate sequel we learn that Judah, now chastened, returns to his brethren.[1]

Like his ancestor Judah, Elimelech, our man from Bethlehem in Judah, has left his home to sojourn among foreigners, not intending originally to settle. Significantly, he seems to have chosen idolatrous Moab and its uncultivated or wild spaces as an arena where he might live more easily as a stranger. Accompanying him are his wife and his two sons. After we get everyone's name—more on this in a moment—we are told, again, "they came to the field of Moab," and, moreover, "they were there": although Elimelech intended but to sojourn, he decided to remain. Three questions occur to us: Why did he leave? Why go to Moab? Why stay there? Once again, the text is silent; once again, we can take silence as an invitation to speculate.

Why did the man leave his homeland? Was he escaping the wrongdoing of his fellows that gave rise to social disorder and the famine (just as, in Genesis, Judah escaped the wrongdoing of his brothers in their attack on Joseph)? If so, was it irresponsible of him not to stay and help them deal with the crisis? Was it improper for him to forsake his people, his land and way of life, and even his God? Should we also (or instead) see his act of abandonment as an emblem of the waywardness of the entire people, of their propensity to chase after false gods? Or, to the contrary, was Elimelech, like his ancestors (Abraham, followed by Judah and his brothers) who went down to Egypt during a famine, justifiably going to the one place where he might feed his family? If so, was the man also justified in choosing to go to *Moab*, and to stay there? What is Moab and who are the Moabites?

Moab was the land to the east of the Jordan River and Dead Sea, just across the water from the territory belonging to the tribe of Judah. Like the descendants of the eponymous Judah, the Moabites also had unsavory beginnings. The original Moab (*mo'av*; "of his father") was born of the incestuous union that the elder of Lot's two daughters perpetrated on their drunken father following their flight from the utter destruction of Sodom and Gomorrah (Genesis 19:30–38). Not only for this ancestral reason but also for their own moral failings, the Moabites later became permanent *personae non gratae* in Israel—indeed, the very embodiment of everything anti-Israelite. As the Hebrews freed from Egyptian bondage approached the Promised Land toward the end of their forty-year sojourn in the wilderness, Balak, the king of Moab, summoned the prophet Balaam to curse them and thereby obtain their destruction (Numbers 22–24). In addition, Moabite women, given to licentious practices, seduced many Israelites from the neighboring encampment while simultaneously inducing them to go whoring after Baal and other pagan gods (Numbers 25:1–3). Finally, the Moabites refused the Israelites sustenance and safe passage at this critical final juncture of their wanderings. Thus, as they neared the Promised Land, Moses laid down the law, singling out the iniquitous Moabites—along with the Ammonites, descendants of Ammon, born of the incestuous union of Lot's *younger* daughter with her drunken father—for special condemnation:

> An Ammonite or a Moabite shall not enter into the assembly of the Lord; even to the tenth generation shall none of them enter into the assembly of the Lord forever; because they met you not with bread and with water in the way, when you came forth out of Egypt; and because they hired against you Balaam the son of Beor from Pethor of Aramnaharaim, to curse you. Nevertheless the Lord your God would not hearken to Balaam; but the Lord your God turned the curse into a blessing to you, because the Lord your God loved you. You shall not seek their peace or their prosperity all your days forever. (Deuteronomy 23:4–7)

In nearby passages, Moses allows that the spite-filled Edomites (descendants of Esau) and even the enslaving Egyptians may be permitted, albeit only after three generations, to marry into the Israelite community; but a vile Moabite, never.

Readers who know this Mosaic teaching will be shocked to learn in the Book of Ruth that the man from Bethlehem chooses first to sojourn and then to remain—with unmarried sons—among the Moabites. Elimelech not only forsakes his people in time of need. He not only abandons the land of God's covenant. He embraces the eternal enemy of the Lord's people and of the Lord Himself. Whatever his intentions or motives, he becomes in effect an idolater. As we will soon see, he also becomes a failure.

A clue to his destiny can perhaps be found in his name and in the names he gave his sons. "Elimelech" has a pious meaning: "my god (*'El-i*) is king (*melekh*)." But it can just as easily be glossed impiously and understood arrogantly: "to me (*'el + i*), [let] the king[ship] [come]." Unhappy not only with the famine but with the form of rule in his native land, and perhaps (for these reasons) disaffected also from the God of Israel, Elimelech moves away to the anti-Israel in search of greener political and religious fields of fortune. But Elimelech's prospects for reaping those fields and leaving his mark on the world are undercut by the names this self-serving man gives his sons: Mahlon means "sickly" (from *machalah*, "sickness"), and Chilion means "vanishing" (from *kalah*, "to cease [to be]"). Prophetically, the names of the sons anticipate their early demise and their childlessness: the subject of the next verses.

Arrayed against these ominous (masculine) names, we have only the hope-filled name of Elimelech's wife, Naomi: *na'omi*, "my delight." In the world of men, Naomi at first remains in the background. It will take the death of her husband and her sons for Naomi to capture our attention. Despite her great loss, she will remain a delight to all who know her.

> And Elimelech, Naomi's husband, died; and she
> was left behind (*vatisha'er*; from *sha'ar*, "to remain
> or be left alone"), and her two sons. And they took
> them wives of the women of Moab: the name of the
> one was Orpah, and the name of the other Ruth;
> and *they dwelt there about ten years*. And died both
> of them, Mahlon and Chilion; and the woman
> [Naomi] was left behind (*vatisha'er*), [bereaved]
> of her two children and of her husband. (1:3–5;
> emphasis added)

The death of Elimelech, now glossed as (merely) the husband of Naomi, is reported immediately after we learn that "they remained" in the field of Moab. Elimelech dies not of old age or of illness, but as a swift punishment—perhaps for having left the land, perhaps for his arrogance and faithlessness, but perhaps especially for having decided to cast his lot with the Moabites, the nation that once sought to curse the Lord's people. The curse now falls instead on Elimelech and his progeny. Alas, Naomi, the delightful one, is "left behind," a widow with her two sons.

The theme of female solitude is introduced early, but at first Naomi still has her boys. Somewhat surprisingly, they all remain in Moab. Learning nothing from their father's sudden death, the sons unwittingly dig themselves Moabite graves by marrying Moabite women: Mahlon's wife is named Ruth (a name that some have related to *ra'ah*, "to befriend," others to *ra'ah* "to see" and to *re'uth*, "vision"); Chilion's wife is named Orpah ("gazelle," but also perhaps related to 'oref, "back" or "re-treat," prefiguring her "going back" to her people, and "neck" or even "stiff-necked," meaning "not taking the yoke"). Strangely, we are not given the least descrip-tion of the young women, not even of their appearance. Are they beautiful? Are they noble? Are they loving and kind? We must wait and see. For now, we know only their Moabite origins. We will see that their deeds, rather than their looks, will tell us who they are.

Readers are next given a critical fact whose signifi-cance for the larger story is usually overlooked. This little party—Naomi, her two sons and their Moabite wives—has remained in the land *for roughly ten years*; they have had no intention of returning to their home-land. Yet, after this decade in Moab, both of Naomi's sons also die, again leaving her behind, now fully alone, bereaved of both her children and her husband.

Stunned by the news, readers will likely wonder why Mahlon and Chilion both die. Are they taken because of their father's iniquity in abandoning his people, his land, and his God, to join with the Moabites: "For I *Y-H-V-H* your God am a jealous God, visiting the iniq-uities of the fathers upon the sons unto the third or fourth generation of them that hate me, but showing *chesed* unto the thousandth generation of them that love Me and keep My commandments" (Exodus 20: 5–6)? Are they punished for their own refusal to return and for compounding the error by taking Moabite wives? Or are their deaths not at all punitive, but simply needed to set up the dramatic situation required for the rest of the story: the problem of childlessness and the obligation to raise up seed to the deceased?[2]

The text's focus, however, is not on the sons but on Naomi, who—we are twice told, but with great understatement—was "left behind."[3] Having had to witness the deaths and bury the remains of her husband and both her sons, the stricken woman might well be wondering why she is being punished to survive them. She may even feel guilty for the widowed fate of her daughters-in-law. Yet by emphasizing only the fact of Naomi's *solitude*, the text cries out for us to ask not why the sons died, but why they died *childless*. Where are the grandchildren? Ten years of marriage and no children?! *Why* no children from these two marriages?

Some commentators suggest that the childlessness represents divine punishment for the intermarriage, as well as for the decision to embrace the land—and the gods?—of Moab: anyone who departs from God's Way will be cut off from His people. Others suggest that the men were sterile, in keeping with the famine that was afflicting their native land. Still others propose that the absence of progeny symbolically conveys to the reader the future-abolishing meaning of sowing one's seed in foreign soil, especially when sexual indulgence is divorced from its procreative meaning. For the Israelites, Moab *means* a dead end.

Be the reason what it may, the facts of male death and (especially) of female childlessness set up the crucial themes of the rest of the story: female solitude and abandonment and their possible remedy in female solidarity and friendship; female childlessness and its possible remedy in remarriage; and the need for levirate marriage, an obligation hard to fulfill when there is no one left to raise up sons to his dead siblings. Looking ahead, we should not be surprised to find that Naomi, the woman who outlives her children to suffer great grief and shame, later emerges as the apostle of marriage and procreation.

Naomi Decides to Return

The prologue to our story has produced three childless widows—abandoned, bereaved, and unprotected. What will become of them? Where will they go? The answers lie mainly with Naomi, now the center of the story.

> Then she arose with her daughters-in-law (*khallotheha*), that she might return (*vatashav*) from the field of Moab; for she had heard in the field of Moab how that the Lord had remembered (*paqad*) His people in giving them bread. And she went forth out of the place where she was, and her two daughters-in-law [went] with her; and they went on the way to return (*lashuv*) to the land of Judah. (1:6–7)

Naomi is down but she is not out. Until now a passive follower of her husband and, after his death, presumably also of her sons, Naomi is forced—and perhaps spurred—by their demise to take charge. From now on she will not be passive again. There being no future for her widowed self in Moab, unhappy land where her loved ones died, she rises up—from her period of mourning? from her grief?—to return "from the field of Moab," that is, to return to her homeland.

We pause over these first appearances of the pregnant verb, "to return" (*shuv*). It occurs fourteen times in the Book of Ruth, twelve of them in the first chapter, and we will watch it closely. Although it refers primarily to physical homecoming—and Naomi will soon recommend such returns also to her daughters-in-law—it can also be used to describe various re-turnings and homecomings of the soul, most notably repentance (*teshuvah*), a return to life, to wholeheartedness, to God, and to His Way. Naomi at this point is homeless in more ways than one. It remains to be seen if and how—and through whom—she will accomplish a full return.

Now might be a propitious time for Naomi to return to Bethlehem: she has heard rumors that the famine back home has ended, "that the Lord has remembered (*paqad*) His people"—a subtle allusion to the Lord's having "remembered" the childless Sarah (Genesis 21:1–2) and a forward-looking hint of a link between the relief of drought and the relief of barrenness.[4] Perhaps there will now be food for her there, to be gathered from the gleanings left for the poor. Perhaps she can even make a life for herself among her own people. The end of the famine back home makes it *possible* to think of returning. But it quickly becomes evident that Naomi has a different reason for *wanting* to leave: the wellbeing of her daughters-in-law. It is largely for *their* sake that Naomi wants to return and, as we learn immediately, to return *alone*.

A linguistic subtlety foretells an obstacle to her desire. As we shall soon have reason to emphasize, the Hebrew word for "daughter-in-law" is the same as the word for "bride," *kallah*. A woman's relation to the mother or father of her husband is, in an important sense, also as a bride: in patrilineal societies, she is in effect married also to *them*. The "marital" relation persists, as here, even after the husband dies. In the case of Naomi, this "bridal" attachment to the mother-in-law turns out to be especially remarkable, a tribute to her special character. Separation, we are forewarned, will not be easy.[5]

As Naomi sets out on the road to Judah, the young women keep her company. But Naomi soon realizes that they are not just courteously seeing her off. Attached to her in shared familial grief and devoted to her for her noble character, they mean to travel with Naomi all the way—the precise result she wishes to avoid. Speaking for the first time (in a book in which conversation is always the heart of the action), Naomi gives voice to her deepest concerns. We strain to hear her heartfelt words, as we get our first glimpse also of her character.

> And Naomi said to her two daughters-in-law: "Go (*lekhnah*), return (*shovnah*), each of you to *her mother's* house (*'ishah leveth 'immah*); the Lord perform loyal devotion (or "gracious kindness," *chesed*) to you, as you have performed with the dead, and with me. The Lord grant you that you may find *rest* (*menuchah*), each of you in the *house of her husband* (*'ishah beth 'ishah*)." Then she kissed them; and they lifted up their voice, and wept. (1:8–9; emphasis added)

Naomi makes a winning first impression, mainly for her selfless regard for Ruth and Orpah. She understands that the young Moabite widows could have no life in Israel. They would be permanent outcasts, and—save for their relation to her—forever alone: unprotected, impoverished, unmarried, childless, and despised. Concerned for their future welfare, Naomi wants them not to suffer additionally on her account. She urges them to break their tie to her as mother-in-law and to return home each to her own mother—to become again a marriageable daughter in her mother's house, rather than a widowed daughter-in-law living in exile with her. With the name of *Y-H-V-H* twice on her lips, Naomi prays that He will thereafter practice loyal devotion ("gracious kindness," *chesed*) to them by leading them to find rest (*menuchah*) in the *homes* of *new* husbands, husbands whom He will furnish them back home.

We should consider Naomi's words carefully. They not only bespeak her deepest wishes for her daughters-in-law; they may also reveal Naomi's wisdom about womanliness. Why does she wish them each to return to her *mother's* house—not her *father's* house? Why does she pray that each will subsequently find *rest* in the house of her *husband*? Most important, what is the meaning of "rest"—*menuchah*—in this context and why does it require residing in the home of a husband?

A bereaved young widow, especially in patrilineal societies, must disconnect from her in-laws and return to the home of her girlhood if she is to become eligible again to be a bride. Moreover, she needs this return especially in order to heal the wounds of her loss. Like the girl she had been before her marriage, she requires the comfort and understanding of her mother who, much better than her father, would be able to empathize and give counsel and support.[6]

Maternal empathy and support, however, are not yet repose. They provide no remedy for the inarticulate but natural restlessness of an unmarried and childless young woman, who, whether she knows and feels it or not, is unsettled and incomplete until she is married and, especially, a mother of her own children. Only if settled into marriage and motherhood, protected by her husband and fulfilled by giving birth and renewing life out of her own substance, can a woman, according to Naomi, be fully at peace with herself. Only then does she realize nature's silent aspiration for her as woman: to be "the mother of all living" (Genesis 3:20). All other conditions of her existence are rest-less; whether she recognizes it or not, her womanliness craves *menuchah*.[7]

The attainment of *menuchah*—of marital-maternal relief from restlessness—Naomi sees as a gift from the Lord, arriving as an act of divine grace or loyal devotion, of God's *chesed*. In this first appearance of this crucial term—there will be two more in subsequent chapters—Naomi summons the Lord's *chesed* as a reward to her daughters-in-law for their *chesed* to the dead—to Mahlon and Chilion—and to her. The gracious fruitfulness of marriage, implies Naomi, is itself the fruit of loyalty and devotion. *Chesed* begets *chesed*.[8]

A gracious thought, this, on the part of Naomi, especially when we remember that the Lord's *chesed* is generally held to be reserved only for His people and, among them, only for those who love Him and keep His commandments. Speaking perhaps better than she knows, Naomi implies that the extraordinary *chesed* of her Moabite daughters-in-law can move God to rain gracious kindness also upon them, relieving their unmitigated restlessness through the gift of husbands—but only if they return to their own land. Naomi does not yet see that Ruth's remarkable *chesed* is needed back in Naomi's homeland, where it will prove capable of inspiring God to shower His grace not only on her but also, through her, on the entire nation.

Having finished speaking, Naomi kisses her daughters-in-law goodbye, and the three women lift up their voices in shared grief and shed tears of sorrow at the thought of their impending separation. We readers, imagining the scene, also get moist eyes. But the young women, still weeping, protest Naomi's decision and plead with her to take them with her: "No, but we will return (*nashuv*) with you, to your people" (1:10).

Gently but firmly, Naomi again orders them to return, this time making clear her reasons:

> And Naomi said: "Turn back, *my daughters*; why will you go with me? Have I yet sons in my womb, that they may be your husbands? Turn back, *my daughters*, go your way; for I am too old to have a husband. If I should say: 'I have hope,' should I even have a husband tonight, and also bear sons; would you tarry for them till they were grown? Would you shut yourselves off for them and have no husbands? No, *my daughters*; *for it grieves me much for your sakes*, for the hand of the Lord is gone forth against *me*." And they lifted up their voice, and wept again. (1:11–14a; emphasis added)

Naomi speaks intimately and lovingly to the two women. The text, speaking disinterestedly, has (correctly) called them "her daughters-in-law," but Naomi, playing substitute mother, calls them—three times—"my daughters." It is entirely for their sakes *as her daughters* that she now grieves and orders them to return—to cease to be her daughters-*in-law* (her "brides"). She is powerless to provide them the one thing needful: new husbands, to replace those—her sons—whom the Lord has taken from them and from her. Naomi has no living sons who can perform for the deceased Mahlon and Chilion the levirate duty with Ruth and Orpah. Being old, she has no way of getting new sons in the future. Fantasizing to the contrary, she drives home the point: even if she could miraculously find a husband who would impregnate her with sons that very night, would the two young women be willing to wait until the boys were born and reared to adulthood? These blameless and kind young women, insists Naomi, should not have to remain spouseless, unprotected, and childless just because the Lord has come down hard on *her*. (We note, in passing, that Naomi feels godforsaken; her despair has estranged her from *Y-H-V-H*. What, we wonder, will it take for Naomi to return also to Him?) Their only hope is to separate from her and to return to their own homes in Moab. For *their* sake (in the words of Maurice Samuel), she has attempted "to take an everlasting farewell of these beloved links to the beloved dead."[9]

Once again, the three women lift up their voices in pain and shed tears of parting. This time, however, Naomi's words reach their mark with one of the young widows—but not with the other. Both hear the same words, but they respond according to their different natures or characters:

> And Orpah kissed her mother-in-law; but Ruth cleaved to her (*davqah bah*). And she [Naomi] said [to Ruth]: "Behold, your sister-in-law is gone back

to her people, and *to her god(s)* (*'eloheha*); return you
after your sister-in-law." (1:14b–15; emphasis added)

Orpah has gotten the message. She kisses Naomi goodbye and, living out her name, shows us her back (*'oref*)
and returns to her home. No one can fault her. She
makes a decent and sensible choice in favor of homeland and the chance of remarriage and family, against
the certainty of exile and the overwhelming probabil-
ity of lifelong solitude. But about such decent women,
books are not written. Fourteen verses into the story
of her sister-in-law, Orpah leaves the scene, never to be
heard from again.[10]

Ruth makes the opposite choice. Not only does she
remain; she remains firmly attached to Naomi. The
Hebrew verb, here translated "cleaved," *davaq*, denotes
intense personal loyalty and exclusive psychic—indeed,
physical—closeness. It was first used in the Garden of
Eden story to describe the (exogamous, that is, non-inces-
tuous) marital attachment of man and wife: "Therefore
a man leaves his father and mother and *cleaves* (*davaq*)
to his wife, and *they* shall be as one flesh" (Genesis 2:24;
emphasis added). Moses uses the same verb several times
in Deuteronomy, exhorting the Israelites to cleave to—
to remain exclusively loyal and attached to—the Lord.[11]
We will later see that cleaving to someone you love may
be related to cleaving to the Lord.

We are not told why Ruth chooses to stay and why
she cleaves to Naomi. Several possible motives suggest
themselves.

Ruth may be moved by necessity, feeling that she has
no other hope. Having married Mahlon and joined his

family, Ruth might by now have burned her Moabite bridges; returning to her people would not be a viable option. Alone and disheartened after Mahlon's death, Ruth has in Naomi the sole link to her lost love. Indeed, Naomi is in all respects all that is left to her. Thus, Ruth clings to her from loneliness and desperation.

Alternatively, Ruth may be moved by charity. Not her own isolation and misery but Naomi's is what stirs Ruth's soul. Ruth has lost a husband; but Naomi has lost a husband and both of her sons. She is old; she is needy; she is vulnerable. Thus, Ruth clings to her from compassion and empathy.

Finally, Ruth may be moved by genuine love for Naomi, a love based partly on familiarity, partly on shared grief and deepened by sorrow, but mostly on Naomi's lovability, for Naomi is goodness itself. Ruth has lived with her mother-in-law for ten years. She has grown accustomed to her presence and enjoyed her company; she has experienced her kindness; she has witnessed (as here) her selflessness and admired her many virtues. Thus, Ruth clings to Naomi out of friendship— from love and admiration for her person.

These motives are not mutually exclusive. Ruth's choice could be inspired by them all. She and Naomi share in loss and grief; both mourn the same man, one as bereaved mother, one as bereaved widow. Naomi is all Ruth has in the world. Naomi is in need of Ruth's sympathy and care. But even before we hear Ruth speak her heart, we suspect that her cleaving to Naomi bespeaks something remarkable about *both* women: Ruth's great capacity for love and loyal devotion, and Naomi's great worthiness to receive them. Willing to forgo the possibility of one-flesh unity with a man, Ruth *cleaves* to Naomi as if to a husband.

Naomi—her worthiness clearly on display—tries one last time to persuade Ruth to leave her. This time she introduces a theological consideration. She urges Ruth to imitate her sister-in-law who, Naomi pointedly tells her, has returned not only to her people but also to her *god(s)*. At stake in this choice, Naomi wants Ruth to know, is her entire way of life, including her relationship to the divine.

Why does Naomi call attention to this theological difference? Presumably, although we cannot be sure, Ruth had already abandoned her Moabite gods in entering the mixed marriage with Mahlon, a follower (at least nominally) of the Lord (*Y-H-V-H*). But that religious change, Naomi now implies, Ruth would do well to reverse. As Naomi has just told the two women, the Lord has had it in for her, and He is unlikely to treat Ruth any better as long as she remains with Naomi: Ruth would do well to follow a god less hostile to fertility and children than *Y-H-V-H*. Naomi may also be trying to spare Ruth the burdens of a "full conversion" and the extraordinary moral and ritual demands that *Y-H-V-H* places upon His people. Finally, she also wants to spare Ruth the ostracizing animosity that the Israelites have been ordered to display toward the Moabites and, in particular, the prohibition of marriage into the community—a prohibition Naomi fears the community would strictly enforce against Ruth. (Ruth's prospect for re-marriage, we recall, remains the first thing on Naomi's mind.) Hence, Ruth should return to her own gods, who may better prosper her than will *Y-H-V-H*.

Against this reading, some traditional commentators have suggested that Naomi is a proselytizer for the Lord and that, in urging Ruth to leave her, she therefore cunningly has in mind the very opposite intention. Using reverse psychology, and holding up as a bad example the deed of Orpah, she hopes (according to this line of reasoning) to shame Ruth into staying with her and becoming a proselyte for the Lord: Did you see what your sister-in-law did? She turned her back on the Lord and returned to her pagan ways. Do you want to be like her? Do you really want to return to Moabite decadence and immorality?

Such a reading says more about the reader than about Naomi. It may be plausible in the abstract, but it does not fit what's in the text and especially what we know of Naomi. It assumes, without evidence, that Naomi has not only remained devoted to the Lord, despite the severe blows that, as she says, she has received at His hand. It also assumes, again without evidence, that she herself is an active proselytizer, concerned mainly not with the marital happiness of her daughters-in-law but with their religious "conversion." We ourselves see nothing in the text to support this interpretation.

The entire notion of "conversion" in this context is, in fact, an anachronism. Although Jewish tradition will later make much of Ruth's "conversion," there is no basis for the idea or the practice in the Bible or, historically, in biblical times. There is *assimilation* into other cultures, and therewith presumably the de-facto adoption of that culture's religious practices and rituals. But a formal and explicit embrace of a different god—or a formal acceptance of a different "creed"—became an issue for the Jewish people only centuries later, after other religions demanded conversion of *them*. It is only then that the rabbis sought to find precedent for it in the Hebrew Bible. Ruth was the ideal case, waiting, so to speak, to be appropriated for this purpose.

Anything but a proselytizer, Naomi does not even have a favorable or reverent word to say for the Lord. Moreover, as a woman in grief, she speaks painfully and directly from the heart, without the detachment required for calculating intent. As we will see momentarily, Naomi receives Ruth's insistence on joining her not with pious satisfaction but with maternal resignation. Far from seeking her daughter-in-law's "conversion," she is consumed by sadness for Ruth's solitude and concern for her lack of marital prospects. The compassionate Naomi most wants for Ruth a husband and children, not the Lord God of Israel. Indeed, she urges her to abandon the latter for the sake of the former. Naomi cannot at this point foresee how human love and the love of God may be related to each other. She will learn this from Ruth's conduct.

Ruth Speaks Her Heart

Ruth will not be dissuaded from her decision. In answer to Naomi's final plea, Ruth utters the magnificent words of love and loyalty for which she—and the entire book—are justly famous.

> And Ruth said: "Entreat me not to leave you, and to return (*lashuv*) from following after you; for wherever you go, I will go (*telkhi 'elekh*); and where you

lodge (*talini*; from *lun*), I will lodge; your people
(*'am*) shall be my people, and your god(s) (*'elohim*)
my god(s); where you die, I will die, and there will I
be buried; *Y-H-V-H* do so to me, and more also, if
anything but death part you and me." (1:16–17)

For generations upon generations of readers, ourselves included, Ruth's speech stands as the perfect expression of loving and devoted friendship. Her words,
no matter how often we hear them, send our souls soar-
ing. We fall in love with Ruth's nobility, her wholeheartedness, her courage, her resolve, and her simple
eloquence. Yet the speech, grand though it is, does not
stand alone. It exists in a larger context to which it must
be related and against which its significance must finally
be judged. Occurring merely three-fourths of the way
through the first of the book's four chapters, it presents
the book's first word on love and friendship but hardly
its last. We do it no harm if we slow down, analyze its
contents, and see how it fits with what came before and
what comes next.

The big picture is clear: Ruth insists on being allowed
to stay with Naomi. She is not afraid to abandon her
home and her Moabite gods. She is not deterred by
thoughts of being a despised alien in Israel or by burdens of becoming a follower of *Y-H-V-H*. And, as her
answer makes clear, she is definitely not put off by the
idea—emphasized again and again by Naomi—that she
may never marry again. On the contrary, this daughter-in-law (*kallah*)—whom Naomi calls "my daughter"—delivers a set of vows that a bride (*kallah*) would
make (only) to her groom, right down to "until death

do us part." Having earlier joined herself to Naomi's son, Ruth now "espouses" herself to Naomi: to cleave to her wherever she goes, wherever she lodges, wherever she abides. Speaking not as a daughter-in-law or even as a daughter but as a "bride," she will live and die attached to Naomi, and *therefore* also to Naomi's people and even to Naomi's god(s). Also like a spouse, she will be buried at her side. And when Ruth solemnly invokes (for the first time) the Lord God of Israel (not the *'elohim* of Moab), it is not in expression of reverence or in prayer for a blessing. She invokes Him only to call down His punishment on her—misery like yours, Naomi, and more so—should she allow anything but death to separate them.

Two large matters invite comment: the first regards love and friendship. Because, as we have noted, Ruth's words of endearment resemble those of a loving bride, not a few contemporary critics have seen her speech as a declaration of homoerotic love. But there is not a shred of evidence in the text—not here, not later—to support such a sexualized reading. There is nothing of sexual longing in Ruth's heartfelt speech to Naomi. On the contrary, her words bespeak a profound desire—and capacity—for loyal and devoted friendship, that life-long being-together of souls that, as much as is possible and beyond any mere concourse of bodies, can overcome the isolation and separation of human beings. What Ruth promises to Naomi is the rare sort of friendship based not on pleasure or utility but mainly on virtue, originating in admiration, affection, and goodwill for each other and flourishing in the sharing of life's journey together. Naomi had urged Ruth to adhere to her own gods in the hope they would bring her a new husband. Ruth counters by promising adherence only to Naomi: Despite your miseries and embittered lot, despite your dried-up womb, despite your accursed and god-forsaken life, I love and admire your soul and your very being, and I pledge my life to be with you forever. It is a sad commentary on our time that we cannot accept at face value even the possibility—never mind celebrating the grandeur—of such an exalted same-sex but non-sexual relationship.

Some readers, feeling the great passion in Ruth's speech, will balk at using the word "friendship" for the relationship she proposes. Friendship, they hold, is an emotionally cooler love. Friends do not swear undying devotion. Only lovers cleave; friends keep a respectful distance. But intense friendships between women (and even some rare friendships between men, like those between David and Jonathan or Achilles and Patroclus) are anything but emotionally tepid. Lifelong mutual devotion at the highest level will never be common, but even people who have not personally experienced such friendship have long admired its emotional intensity and recognized it as precious.[12] At the same time, however, we must not automatically conclude that the Bible is endorsing the relationship that Ruth so beautifully proposes to Naomi. For we may not assume that Ruth here speaks for the biblical author, any more than we can assume that Macbeth speaks for Shakespeare when he asserts that life "is a tale told by an idiot, full of sound and fury, signifying nothing." Ruth is speaking (only) for herself, albeit in gorgeous words that the biblical author has indeed written for her. What that author *thinks* about Ruth's words—whether he *prefers* loving friendship to marriage and procreation—we must wait and see.

The second theme concerns religious identity and the divine. What is the theological significance of Ruth's speech and her declaration to return with Naomi? Is this in fact an act of "conversion," tacit if not explicit, to the worship of the Lord God of Israel and to joining His people? Naomi had introduced the subject of the divine, first, by praying that *Y-H-V-H* be kind and generous to her daughters-in-law; second, by asserting that *Y-H-V-H* had forsaken her and struck her down; and finally, by urging Ruth to return to her own "gods." (Note her polytheistic assumption.) But in refusing Naomi's directive, Ruth declines to take the theological hint, one way or the other. Instead, she expresses her wholehearted devotion to *Naomi*. It is Naomi, not God, who is emphatically the object of Ruth's piety and devotion: the word "you"—meaning Naomi—occurs six times in Ruth's two sentences; the word "your" occurs twice more.

It is true that Ruth also pledges that Naomi's people and Naomi's god will become her own. Yet in both cases, it seems that those loyalties derive from their being Naomi's: *your* people and *your* god will be mine, but only because they are *yours*. Being *yours*, they are, of course, encompassed in my great love for *you*.

We know nothing of the theological attachments of Elimelech and his sons during their time in Moab, though we suspect they may have wandered off along with the move. We therefore know nothing of the religious commitments of the intermarried couples in the second generation, although, during the decade before the Israelite husbands died, they apparently lived comfortably and well among the Moabites. Traditional readers like to assume that Mahlon and Chilion remained devoted to the God of Israel and that their wives already accepted Him as their own. But that may be wishful thinking. And, in any case, Israelite religious coloration of these "mixed marriages" would have been moot in Moab, there being no Israelite community or religious activity to join. Ruth's religious and national attachments will become an issue only back in Judah; and so she makes clear to Naomi that she will adopt those of her beloved mother-in-law and friend—again, because they are dear to *her*.

None of this looks much like religious conversion—and we have already noted that to speak of "conversion" in this period is itself an anachronism. Yet some might adduce one bit of evidence to suggest that Ruth has already "accepted" the Lord God of Israel. After speaking of "your god" becoming also "my god" and using for this purpose the non-specific (and grammatically plural) Hebrew word *'elohim*, she invokes the name of *Y-H-V-H*, the God of Israel, calling on Him to inflict great misery upon her should she renege on her promise of fidelity to Naomi. In keeping with what Naomi had said about the misery inflicted on her by the Lord, Ruth, too, invokes Him not as a source of blessing but only, should she part from Naomi, as a source of punishment—to do to her what He has already done to Naomi. If this is Israelite piety, it is at best highly partial and poorly informed.

Will the love of Ruth and Naomi bear theological fruit? Will the Lord God of Israel look favorably on Ruth's pious devotion to Naomi? Will Ruth's love for

Naomi restore the latter's faith in God? It will be very interesting to see what "religious" changes may occur, in both Ruth and Naomi, as the story progresses.

Naomi Returns to Bethlehem

As befits its eloquence, Ruth's speech is a conversation stopper. But as befits the human situation, we expect to hear a word from Naomi in response to her daughter-in-law's vow of permanent attachment—if not a word of praise, at least a word of gratitude. Instead, we are treated to silence.

> And when she [Naomi] saw that she [Ruth] was obstinately minded to go with her, she ceased speaking to her. So they two went until they came to Bethlehem. (1:18–19a)

Naomi remains silent not because she is pleased that Ruth will join her or because she is persuaded to accept Ruth's declaration of abiding friendship. She is silent because further argument would be useless. Ruth is adamant; Naomi yields, out of resignation. Ruth appears to have won the day; in truth, however, Naomi has not surrendered. The two women walk in silence, perhaps all the way to Bethlehem, a trip taking more than a week. Each has much on her mind.

Only after they arrive in Bethlehem do we hear Naomi speak, and then only upon provocation.

> And it happened (*vayehi*), when they were come to Bethlehem, that all the city was astir concerning them, and the women said: "Is this Naomi?"

And she said to them: "Call me not Naomi, call me
Marah (*mara'*, "bitterness" [from *mar*, "bitter"]); for
the Almighty (*shadday*) has dealt very bitterly with
me. I went out full, and the Lord has brought me
back ("caused me to return," *heshivani*; causative of
shuv) empty (*reqam*); why call you me Naomi, seeing
the Lord has testified (*'anah*) against me, and the
Almighty has afflicted me?" (1:19b–21)

Once again that word *vayehi*, "it happened." We are
put on alert for trouble. The trouble this time is social.
Naomi's return to Bethlehem, after more than ten years'
absence, causes a sensation: the wife of the prosperous
Elimelech, who left us in the time of famine, returns
a pauper, a mere shadow of her former self. Eyeing her
up and down, the women cannot believe what they see:
can this really be Naomi? Their attitude, we suspect, is
not empathetic but unfeeling—or worse: that's what she
gets for having left us in time of trouble; see how the
mighty have fallen. We observe that the women of Bethlehem take no notice of the presence of Ruth: is this an
intentional slight of an obvious foreigner, or are they so
focused on Naomi as to overlook the younger woman's
presence?

Naomi, miserable but with pride intact, cuts through
the silent condescension. Standing up to the women,
she offers her own declaration of defeat and despair. She
rejects her name, "my delight," in favor of "bitterness,"
a bitterness she blames on the Almighty who "has dealt
very bitterly with me." Her evidence: I went out full,
that is, wealthy and blessed with husband and sons; but
the Lord has brought me back empty, that is, old and

barren, worn and weary, impoverished, widowed, and childless. Why, she protests, do you still call me Naomi, when, as you see, the Lord has testified against me (or, "has humbled me"), punishing my emigration to Moab with this reversal of fortune? Why do you still call me "my delight" when the Almighty has worsened my lot?

Just as Naomi made no answer to Ruth's declaration of undying devotion, so the women of Bethlehem make no answer to Naomi's declaration of misery. They offer not a word of comfort. They make no offer of assistance. They do not ask about her companion. It is an icy homecoming. The famine may have ended in Bethlehem, but a dearth of *chesed* remains.

Stuck in her own misery, Naomi in fact contributes to the coldness. In claiming that she has returned home empty, she, too, neglects the presence of Ruth and her vow of lasting devotion. Forgotten, too, are Ruth's Moabite origins. Not so the text. In concluding the first chapter, summarizing what has just occurred, the voice of the text immediately and pointedly corrects both omissions:

> So Naomi *returned* (*vatashav*), and Ruth *the Moabitess*, her *daughter-in-law, with her*, who returned (literally, "the [one] returning"; *hashavah*) *out of the fields of Moab*—and they came to Bethlehem in the beginning of barley harvest. (1:22; emphasis added)

Naomi does not return *altogether* "empty." Returning with her was Ruth—the Moabitess—her daughter-in-law (*kallah*)—when she (Naomi? Ruth?) returned out of the fields of Moab. Orpah had returned to her people and her gods; Naomi has now returned to her homeland in Bethlehem. But Ruth, because she chose to cleave to Naomi, is also in an emotional sense a returnee to a land that she has never seen before. She will make of it a home not only for herself but also for her mother-in-law. Indeed, it is Ruth who will bring—return—the despairing Naomi back to life. Alive in Ruth's *chesed*, and unbeknownst to her, the spirit of the Lord will also return to the Promised Land.

Act One is over. It began with prosperous Elimelech's emigration to the field of Moab; it ends with impoverished Naomi's return out of the fields of Moab. The men in her life are dead. In their place is Ruth the Moabitess, her daughter-in-law, her *kallah*. No one offers them assistance; they will have to fend for themselves. The rest of the story depends on the presence of the devoted Moabite woman and on the fact that it is time for the barley harvest—tiny intimations of possible hope. For barley, the first crop to ripen, is a harbinger of the restoration of fertility, not only to the land but also to Naomi and Ruth.

Ruth Gleans in the Field of Boaz

The second chapter immediately thickens the plot. Unbeknownst to the reader, Naomi is not really devoid of kin. Indeed, her kinsman—actually, her husband's kinsman—is a man of distinction.

> And Naomi had a kinsman of her husband's, a mighty man of valor (*'ish gibor chayil*), of the family of Elimelech, and his name was Boaz. (2:1)

The phrase *gibor chayil* usually refers to a mighty warrior, but in this context it conveys nobility of character and (especially) important and prosperous standing in the community: Boaz is a leading man, perhaps *the* foremost man in town. (His name is of uncertain origin. Some suggest that it means "fleetness"; others suggest that it means, "in him is strength," from *bo* and *oz*.) We are pleased to meet him, for we hope that help might be forthcoming from his quarter.

But we are quickly disappointed. We are told of his relation to Naomi and we are told his name, but nothing is said about what he does; big man though he is, he has done nothing worthy of mention for our story. On the contrary, the text's silence proclaims loudly what he hasn't done. Although he is Naomi's kinsman, he has made no effort to see her; although he is a man of means, he has not offered to help. (As we will later learn, Naomi has another kinsman, also well off and even closer to her than Boaz. He, too, has ignored her.)

Boaz cannot plead ignorance of her presence: the whole town has been astir over Naomi's return. *Everyone* knows: Naomi is back and she is destitute and despairing. So where has Boaz been? What has kept him from calling? Why has he not done right by the widow of his kinsman? Are there expectations of him that he does not wish (or is not able) to meet? Is he standoffish because of the Moabite woman with whom Naomi lives? We do not know. For whatever reason, Boaz has been missing in action.

To solve this mystery, and to exonerate Boaz of negligence, traditional commentators have suggested that he has recently lost his wife and is still in mourning. Indeed, one version suggests that Naomi and Ruth have arrived back in Bethlehem during the funeral of Boaz's wife—hence the reason the townswomen are out and about. There is, of course, nothing in the text to support—or to contradict—these suggestions.

Although it does not give us the reason, the text subtly but clearly points up Boaz's negligence. Having introduced him by name, it immediately moves to the dwelling of Naomi and Ruth and lets us see their abject neediness. The two widows are, as Maurice Samuel puts it, "thrown on the social-security system of ancient Judea, which provided that at harvest time the corners of fields and stray ears of grain be left for the poor."[13]

> And said Ruth the Moabitess to Naomi, "Let me now go to the field, and glean (*va'alaqqatah*; from *laqat*, "gather up, collect") among the ears of grain after him in whose sight I shall find favor (*chen be'enayv*)." And she said to her, "Go, my daughter" (*lekhi viti*). (2:2)

It is Ruth who initiates the action. It is the Moabite stranger, and pointedly not the just-introduced kinsman Boaz, who acts to take care of Naomi. Wishing to protect her once prosperous mother-in-law from the humiliations of having to beg or of being seen ignominiously gleaning in the fields of others, Ruth asks permission to do some gleaning herself. Not to worry, she tells Naomi, she will go only where she is welcome, "after him in whose sight I shall find favor." Her remarks, which speak better than she knows, anticipate the possibility that someone might very well take a fancy to her while she is gleaning.

We must pause on the subject of gleaning, an activity central to our story's plot and pregnant with our story's meaning.[14] The practice is rooted in the Lord's commandments at Sinai. Several times in the Torah, the Children of Israel are ordered not to harvest their entire fields or to gather any leavings from the ground. The corners of the field and all fallen crops are to be left for gleaning ("gathering up"; *laqat*) by strangers and the poor (and, in one version of the injunction, also by widows and orphans).[15] This gracious practice of charity toward those lacking their own land to plant and harvest embodies and mirrors a deeper teaching about the land and about ownership.

Just as the Promised Land is a gracious gift from the Lord to the Children of Israel, so what the land produces is a gift to its inhabitants. To be sure, people must till the soil if it is to bring forth its plentiful fruit. But the fertility of the earth precedes human labor and exceeds human merit. Indeed, the land produces generously; it yields more than enough to meet everyone's needs. There is therefore no reason to hoard against tomorrow or to take more than is required to feed your family and livestock; and the abundance also allows you to feed your neighbor and to nourish the larger community. Ownership of land—which ultimately belongs to God—is thus for stewardship, rather than for selfish appropriation and exploitation. (This teaching is embodied also in the commandment about the Sabbatical Year [*shemitah*]: every seven years the land must be allowed to lie fallow and rest, while the poor may feed off its spontaneous productions [Exodus 23:10–11].) Leaving the gleanings of your fields for the stranger and the poor mirrors the grace of the land itself. It is not an accident that the gleaning field turns out to be a fitting

stage for the expression of human *chesed*—and for the
beginning of love.

To return to our story: Naomi immediately agrees
to Ruth's proposal, and not only because she and Ruth
are in need of food. Naomi has not sought outside help.
Although she surely knows of the presence of her late
husband's kinsmen, she has not approached them for
aid—perhaps out of shame for her poverty, perhaps out
of a pride that refuses to beg, but perhaps because she
has in mind a purpose higher than food. Being no fool,
Naomi surely notices the lack of kindred attention and
care; but she says nothing about it to Ruth, not wanting to prejudice her against the man who might yet turn
out to be her redeemer (and also not wanting Ruth to
feel guilty for being the reason—due to her Moabite origins—that others are staying away). So Naomi simply
bides her time and waits for Ruth to take the initiative.
When she does, Naomi does not direct her to Boaz's
field or even mention his existence. Although happy that
Ruth will be out and on view, she does not want to burden Ruth with disturbing knowledge or (especially) with
false hopes. What will be, will be: "Go, my daughter,"
with my gratitude and my blessing.

> And she went, and she came and she gleaned in the
> field after the reapers; and her chance was to happen
> upon the part of the field belonging to Boaz, who
> was of the family of Elimelech. And behold, Boaz
> (*vehinneh vo'az*), he came from Bethlehem, and said
> to the reapers: "The Lord be with you" (*Y-H-V-H
> 'immakhem*). And they answered him: "The Lord
> bless you" (*yevarekhekha Y-H-V-H*). Then said Boaz

to his servant that was set over the reapers: "Whose damsel (*na'arah*; "maiden," "young woman") is this?" (2:3–5)

Fortune—or is it rather providence?—smiles on this gracious but foreign young woman, not once but twice. In going out to glean, she "just happens" to follow the reapers working that portion of the field that "just happens" to belong to Boaz, whom *we* are again told—but *she* does not know—is a relative of Elimelech. While she is gleaning, *mirabile dictu*, Boaz himself "just happens" to appear—not an everyday occurrence on the field. Delightedly, the text exclaims: "Behold, [it is] Boaz." The maid and the master are on stage together. We are all eyes and ears.

However much we have faulted Boaz for his seeming inattention to Naomi, he makes a wonderful first impression now that we meet him in the flesh. This very important man greets his workers with a blessing, "The Lord be with you," as (says the medieval commentator Abraham Ibn Ezra) "an ever-sustaining help in your labors." The first word the reapers—and we readers—hear from Boaz's mouth is the name of the Lord.[16] The reapers respond in kind: "May the Lord bless you," by (Ibn Ezra again) "granting you a rich and abundant crop."

This simple exchange of greetings speaks volumes. It offers proof of, and tacitly expresses gratitude for, the end of the famine. Unlike his wayward kinsman Elimelech, who became one with the earth in Moab, Boaz has stayed in Bethlehem and endured the scarcity. He neither left his people nor lost trust in God. On meeting his men, he straightway puts *Y-H-V-H* into their thoughts, implicitly reminding them that they prosper not solely by the power and might of their own hands.[17] Boaz is more than a wealthy landowner; he leads men to honor God.

But, unlike a wealthy landowner, Boaz does not ask about the harvest. No sooner are greetings exchanged than his eyes land on Ruth. Something about her has caught his attention, perhaps even before he speaks. Was she the only female gleaner out today among the reapers? Unlikely. Was she a newcomer among the regular gleaners? Perhaps. How did she stand out from the others? For what did she find favor in his eyes? Was it her unusual appearance, her (foreign?) dress, her posture or manner, or was it her beauty, her modesty, her grace?[18] And never mind Ruth, in what mood—suspicion or curiosity, distaste or delight, lust or longing?—is Boaz asking? We have no idea. For whatever reason, Boaz presses his overseer to identify her.

The overseer, puzzled or embarrassed or caught off-guard by the question, stammers out a long-winded answer, saying more than was called for:

> "It is a Moabitish damsel, the one that came back with Naomi out of the field of Moab; and she said: 'Let me glean, I pray you, and gather after the reapers among the sheaves'; so she came, and she has continued (*vata'amod*; from *'amad*, "to persist") even from the morning until now, save that she tarried a little in the house." (2:6–7)

What is the overseer trying to say? Perhaps this: Oh, she's no one special, just a Moabite girl. And, if you're struck by her good manners, why, it must be just Naomi's teaching. Or if you're wondering why I let her stay or why she's still here (and I'm not at all happy about it myself), well, she begged me to let her glean after the reapers; I felt I couldn't refuse her—she belongs to Naomi, you know—and, my, what a worker; she's been at it all day—except for a little break that she took in the house.

Or perhaps—in an alternative explanation for his nervous answer—the overseer is embarrassed not for himself but for *Boaz*, and feels the need to hide it: Oh (says the overseer, pretending), you would have no reason to know who she is. She's a young woman, a Moabite maid (not "*the*" Moabite maid), who (as everybody knows, including you) returned with Naomi and who gleans tirelessly all day with almost no rest, because she's very needy and (though I'm too embarrassed to say this outright) Naomi's rich relatives have not come forward to help her.[19]

First Words

Taken with Ruth's appearance and manner and (especially) with the fact that she is humbly gleaning for her mother-in-law—and perhaps impressed also by the overseer's report of her steadfastness, or eager to atone for his neglect of Naomi—Boaz solicitously approaches Ruth. A lovely and delicate conversation ensues, Boaz leading. Grace begets graciousness.

> Then said Boaz to Ruth: "Hear you not, my daughter (*biti*)? Go not to glean in another field, neither pass from this one, but cling (*davaq*; "cleave") here to my maidens (*na'arothay*). Let your eyes be on the

field that they do reap, and go you after them; have
I not charged the young men that they shall not
touch you? And when you are thirsty, go to the ves-
sels, and drink of that which the young men have
drawn." (2:8–9)

Like Naomi when sending her out, Boaz addresses
Ruth familiarly as "my daughter." In speech at once
invitational and directing, he bids her to glean only in
his field, to cling (that word again, *davaq*) only to his
maidservants, and to follow them as they reap. Revealing that he has already taken special pains to protect
her (and thus tacitly acknowledging that, as an attractive young woman, she needs such protection), he lets
her know that she has nothing to fear from his young
men: he has commanded them—or, more likely, is now
commanding them—to leave her alone. He even directs
her to quench her thirst with water that the lads have
drawn for themselves. Boaz is falling all over himself to
make her feel welcome. Displaying more consideration
than either hospitality or atonement for prior neglect
would warrant, he shows interest in Ruth herself, well
beyond what seems reasonable. Ruth, quite fittingly, is
astonished.

Then she [Ruth] fell on her face, and bowed down
to the ground, and said to him: "Why (*madu'a*)
have I found favor in your sight (*chen be'enekha*),
that you should take cognizance of me (*lehakireni*,
from *nakar*, "to recognize"), seeing I am a foreigner
(*nokhriyah*, from *nokhriy*, "stranger" and *nekhar*,
"strange")?" (2:10)

Moved by the master's unusual solicitude, Ruth respectfully and humbly shows him deference and gratitude. With her face to the ground, she modestly conceals her blushing embarrassment at having attracted his special notice. However, Ruth is hardly meek or tongue-tied. Although prostrate on the ground, her first utterance in public is a question seeking understanding, and her first word is *madu'a*, "why." Ruth boldly gives voice to her amazement at his attention and kindness and presses him to explain them; at the same time, she makes clear—indeed, emphasizes—that she is a foreigner (not his "daughter" and, as everybody knows, a Moabite). Artfully, Ruth pushes hard on the relation between *recognition* (as both "knowledge" and "respect") and *familiarity* or its absence, cleverly punning on the distinction and connection between "recognizing" (*nakar*) and "strangeness" (*nekhar*): you surely must discern my foreignness, so why are you extending me recognition?[20] Does not my difference count with you? Do you really mean all this kindness to "foreign me"? Can you have recognized something in me that transcends my foreignness? By boldly rubbing his nose in her alien status, Ruth tacitly puts Boaz's character on trial.

Awash in his own strange emotions and now much taken with Ruth's modesty and her initiative in word and deed, Boaz is grateful for an opportunity to explain himself. Moved by her graciousness, he returns it with interest. Within the hearing of all around, he answers her expansively, making clear to her—and to them and to the reader—that he already knows her remarkable story.

And Boaz answered and said to her: "It has fully
been told me all that you have done for your
mother-in-law since the death of your husband; and
how you have left your father and your mother, and
the land of your nativity, and are come to a people that you knew not before. *Y-H-V-H* recompense your work, and be your reward complete from
Y-H-V-H, the God of Israel, under whose wings
(*kenafav*) you are come to take refuge." (2:11–12)

Boaz's answer is pitch-perfect. Addressing Ruth's sense
of her unworthiness to receive his favors because she is a
foreigner, he ascribes his attentions entirely to her merit.
She has earned his recognition and consideration, he
wants her to know, because of stories he has heard about
her loyal devotion to her mother-in-law in the face of the
death of her husband.[21] This kindness to her mother-in-
law, Boaz appreciates, has come at the price of leaving
her own father and mother and her homeland and of becoming a stranger in a strange land. Yet in his eyes, he
wants her and everyone else around to know, she is no
mere foreigner, never mind a despised Moabite. On the
contrary, she is not defined by her alien birth but by her
choice to come with Naomi to the land of Israel. Says
Boaz (inspired now to speak of the Lord, and echoing
Naomi's similar invocation), her virtuous conduct enti-
tles her to *Y-H-V-H's* blessing (and to His reward for her
work), which he calls down upon her. His own solicitude
for Ruth, he implies, is but a manifestation of the care
of the Lord God of Israel: she has come seeking refuge
under His wings (*tachath kenafav*); she has now found it,
he wants her (and everyone) to know, in his own fields.

A few other things about Boaz's remarks deserve mention. As some readers have observed, his entire speech is a poem, one composed by Boaz on the spot. If Ruth has inspired him to speak ultimately of the Lord, she has also inspired him from the start to speak in verse.[22] The language is elevated; the images resonate with biblical antecedents ("leaving father and mother to cleave to his wife" [Genesis 2:24]; Abraham leaving "his land and his kindred and his father's house" unto the Promised Land [Genesis 12:1]); the speaker's voice soars. Clearly, Boaz has been deeply touched by Ruth. In recognizing and responding to her great goodness, he displays his own.

Not to be overlooked, however, is the reticence of Boaz's reply: he does not introduce himself by name, neither does he identify himself as Naomi's kinsman. Ruth is not to know of his prior neglect (or of the implications of his near kinship). And although speaking poetically in satisfying her concerns, Boaz, ever the *'ish gibbor chayil*, makes no improper advances.

Boaz's remarks achieve their purpose. Ruth is entirely reassured.

> Then she said: "Let me find favor in your sight (*chen be'enekha*), my lord (*'adoni*); for that you have comforted me, and for that you have spoken to the heart (*lev*) of your handmaid, though I be not as one of your handmaidens." (2:13)

Ruth had led with a worry about her foreignness. Boaz has turned it into a virtue: in his version, Ruth has chosen to abandon her alien home and ways and has remade herself as one of the Lord's people. Comforted by his gracious and public acceptance of her presence,

Ruth humbly accepts his attentions, seeing as he has
made her feel like one of his own. Ruth goes off to glean
with the other women. As she leaves, her remark lingers
with the reader: you, Boaz, have touched my heart.

Boaz is not yet finished with her. As the reapers
break for lunch, Ruth sits apart and far off. Boaz, making a public show of his attentions, summons her to par-
take of the food and even to eat at his side.

> And Boaz said to her at mealtime: "Come hither,
> and eat of the bread, and dip your morsel in the
> vinegar." And she sat beside the reapers; and they
> reached her parched grain, and she did eat and was
> satisfied, and left thereof. (2:14)

It is easy to overlook the delicate beauty of this scene.
The foreign handmaiden, still self-conscious of her low
and alien status, shyly keeps her distance from the lunch-
ing reapers. But the master again takes public notice of
her, makes sure that she eats and does not eat alone, and
integrates her into the community of diners, dipping
and all. As she joins them "at table," his men make good
on his gracious offer of hospitality and see to it that food
reaches her. Of Ruth's reaction we are told only, "she did
eat and was satisfied." We are left to imagine how she in-
wardly felt as she left the meal to return to gleaning. Relief, of course. Gratitude, to be sure. But, very likely, also
wonder, puzzlement, and a touch of embarrassment—all
occasioned by Boaz's special attention to her. What did
it really mean? Was there more to it than simple human-
kindness? Why was it coming from him in her direction?

Had she known what happens next, Ruth would have
been even more confused.

And when she had risen up to glean, Boaz commanded his young men, saying: "Let her glean even among the sheaves, and put her not to shame. And also pull out some for her on purpose from the bundles, and leave it, and let her glean, and rebuke her not." (2:15–16)

To increase Ruth's take-home yield, Boaz commands his workers to allow Ruth unusual privileges: she may glean not only in the reaped fields but also among the bound sheaves. More remarkable, they are to remove for her sake stalks of grain from those bundled sheaves. Most importantly, the young men are ordered neither to put Ruth to shame nor to rebuke her for taking advantage of these special privileges. Ruth is not to know that she is receiving Boaz's affirmative action, taken on her behalf. Whether favoring her for her own sake and his own reasons, or whether making up through her for his prior neglect of Naomi, Boaz sees to it that Ruth will have a highly profitable day gleaning. All by himself, Boaz delivers to Ruth the large reward for her labor that he had called upon the Lord to provide.

We readers are deeply touched by the scene we have just witnessed. The Lord's grace often works through human hands, and here grace has elicited grace, which then rewards and elicits grace yet again. *Chesed* is a two-way street. Inspired by Ruth's example, Boaz turns into a giver. The landowner, previously lacking in charity, becomes whole-heartedly a follower of the Lord. From having had *Y-H-V-H* on his tongue, Boaz now has Him more deeply in his heart. This prosperous leading citizen of Bethlehem has embraced in full the biblical teaching of *chesed* regarding the land and the poor or the stranger. Like a true philanthropist, he offers deliberate gifts (not just the right to accidental leavings), while taking pains not to humiliate the recipient. We read on with hopes not only for Ruth and Naomi, but also for a possible redemption of the land that had been so greatly troubled in the days of the judging of judges.

Reporting to Naomi

Boaz may have dropped extra grain, but Ruth did not waste her opportunity. She worked until the sun went down.

> So she gleaned in the field until evening; and she beat out that which she had gleaned, and it was about an ephah of barley. And she took it up, and went into the city; and her mother-in-law saw what she had gleaned; and she brought forth and gave to her that which she had left after she was satisfied. And her mother-in-law said to her: "Where have you gleaned to-day? And where have you worked? —Blessed be he that did take knowledge of you." (2:17–19a)

The yield of the day's gleaning was remarkable: a whole ephah of barley grain, a little more than a bushel (roughly thirty-six liters), an astounding result especially for someone who had never gleaned before and who does not know her way around. Naomi is overjoyed and duly impressed. Suddenly animated, she bursts into speech. Where, she wants to know, did Ruth glean today? Where have you worked? Grateful for this much-needed bounty, even before hearing Ruth's answer Naomi calls down a blessing on the (as yet unnamed) landowner who had allowed her to glean.

Ruth's reply initiates a remarkable conversation between the two women.

> And she told her mother-in-law with whom she had worked; and she said: "The name of the man with whom I worked today [is] Boaz." And Naomi said to her daughter-in-law: *"May he be blessed by Y-H-V-H,* Who has not abandoned His *loyal devotion* (*chesed*) to the living *and to the dead."* And Naomi said to her: "Near to us is the man (*qarov lanu ha'ish*; in other words, "he is our relative"), one of our redeemers (*go'alenu* [from *ga'al,* "to redeem"]) is he." (2:19b–20; emphasis added)

At Ruth's mention of Boaz's name, Naomi's heart skips a beat: This cannot be coincidence. At last! The Lord has taken note of us. For the first time since she returned to Bethlehem, a glimmer of hope appears before Naomi's despairing soul. She gives immediate voice to her gratitude to both Boaz and *Y-H-V-H.* She calls down His blessing on Boaz, in whose act of *chesed* Naomi discerns the *chesed* of the Lord. And not just His loyal devotion to the living: He "has not abandoned His *chesed* to the living *and to the dead."* Ruth, silent, is perplexed: How does my gleaning in Boaz's field show the Lord's devotion, and also *to the dead*? Reading her silence correctly, Naomi reveals what she has in mind: Boaz, your benefactor, is a relative of ours; more than that, he is a near-kinsman or redeemer (literally, "from among our redeemers is he"). What is left unspoken is this: precisely because Boaz is a near-kinsman, he has a right and a duty to redeem us. And should he redeem us, he will be redeeming also our dead husbands.

What is the meaning of "redemption" and what are the duties of the *go'el* or redeemer? We shall have more to say about this later when the redemption actually takes place. Yet given the centrality of this idea for the entire story, we can offer an introductory account.

Although the idea of redemption (*ge'ulah*) as enunciated in the Torah originally involved many things (including the avenging of bloodshed [Numbers 35:9 ff.]), the *go'el*'s major function eventually became preventing the alienation of land from the family. Thus, if a man, having become impoverished, is forced to sell his land to an outsider, he may appeal to his kinsman to redeem it for the family by repurchase. And by biblical commandment, his next of kin is required to do so: "If your brother becomes poor, and sells part of his property, then his kinsman (*go'el*), the one nearest to him, shall come and redeem (*ga'al*) that which his brother has sold" (Leviticus 25:25). The root meaning of the verb, *ga'al*, is "to restore." Thus, redemption (*ge'ulah*) is, at its heart, the restoration of something—especially landed property—to its original condition.

Particularly relevant to our story is a special kind of restoration, if one not generally called *ge'ulah*. This is needed when a man dies without a male heir, jeopardizing both the fate of his property and his name in the community. In the classical case, the situation calls for levirate marriage (*yibbum*), to be performed by one of the *brothers* of the deceased. Moses, in Deuteronomy, prescribes the rite precisely:

> When brothers dwell together and one of them dies and has no child, the wife of the deceased shall not be married outside to a stranger. Her husband's brother (*yevamah*) should go in unto her and take her as his wife and do *yibbum* with her (*veyibemah*). And the eldest son who shall be born [from this levirate union] *will stand upon [represent] the name of the deceased brother* and *his [the deceased brother's] name shall not be erased from Israel.* (Deuteronomy 25:5–6; emphasis added)

The practice accomplishes several things at once. The widow is rescued from widowed isolation and barrenness. The dead husband, through "his" new son (who will inherit his land), is redeemed from anonymity in Israel. The land is not alienated from the family. The brother performing levirate procreation practices *chesed* (loyal devotion) toward his dead brother: truly his brother's keeper, he refuses to acquiesce in—never mind profit from—his brother's disappearing without a trace. He refuses, in other words, metaphorically to re-enact Cain against Abel.

Needless to say, this is a heavy obligation, one that not all brothers will readily accept. A man's own wife and children may suffer; he will have added expense; he may find the widow repugnant or nasty; he may have hated his brother. Acknowledging this fact, the law (grudgingly) allows for exemption, but only through a humiliating procedure (known as *chalitsah*, "removal" [of the shoe]) that permanently stains the name of any man who refuses:

> If the man does not desire to take his sister-in-law (*yevimto*), his sister-in-law shall go up to the elders in the gate and say, "My brother-in-law (*yevami*) refuses to establish for his brother a name in Israel; he does not want to perform *yibbum* with me." Then the elders of his city shall call him, and speak to him; and if he stands, and says "I like not to take her," then shall his brother's wife draw near unto him in the presence of the elders, and remove his shoe from off his foot, and spit in his face; and she shall answer and say: "So shall it be done to the man that does not build up his brother's house." And his name shall be called in Israel "the house of him that had his shoe removed." (Deuteronomy 25:7–10)

The situation we have in the Book of Ruth differs from the classic case: there are no surviving brothers of Mahlon to redeem him and his patrimony. The law of *yibbum* does not apply. But analogous rights and quasi-duties of redemption may fall on near-relatives; it is they alone who can, by marrying the widow, redeem both her and her dead husband. As we shall see, this is not, as with brothers, a binding legal obligation on the near-kinsmen; they will not be publicly humiliated at law should they refuse. Yet the very existence of these relatives holds out hope for such intra-familial—levirate-*like*—redemption. It is this hope of which Naomi speaks. It is this prospect, now vivified by Ruth's (providential?) encounter with Boaz, which brings Naomi back to life.

Ruth has not understood the import of Naomi's remark about the near-kinsman. As the text subtly hints, she continues to think as a Moabite. She glosses Naomi's remark about redemption by emphasizing Boaz's permission to continue her gleaning throughout the entire harvest. But she does so with a pregnant addition of her own.

> And Ruth *the Moabitess* said: "He also said to me: 'To my young men (*na'arim*) you shall cleave (*davaq*), until they have finished all my harvest.'" And Naomi said to Ruth her daughter-in-law: "It is good, my daughter, that you go out with his *maidens* (*na'aroth*), and that you be not met in any other field." So she *cleaved* (*davaq*) to the maidens of Boaz to glean to the end of barley harvest and of wheat harvest; and [or, better, "but"] she *dwelt* (*vateshev*) *with her mother-in-law.* (2:21–23; emphasis added)

We are arrested by the reappearance of the verb to cleave, *davaq*, used first to describe how Ruth, unlike Orpah, acted toward Naomi (1:14) and what she, in effect, promised to do forever (1:16–17). Boaz had in fact instructed Ruth to cleave to his *maidens* and to glean in no other field (2:8). But Ruth now has him telling her to cleave to his *young men*. Did Ruth, her erotic yearnings perhaps awakened, imagine that a husband might be found for her among Boaz's men? Could this be how Boaz would be the kinsman redeemer?

Naomi gently sets her straight but without directly contradicting her. Ruth is not to cleave to the young men; she is to go out rather with the young *women*, with Boaz's maidens (*na'aroth*). And, of course, she is to go to no other field. Naomi wants to keep Ruth in the company of the young women. She is not to arouse their enmity or jealousy by hanging out alone with the men. She is not to arouse the desires or hopes of any young man by her own forward behavior. Naomi, who from the start has been eager to prevent her daughters-in-law from remaining unmarried and childless, has a higher if as yet unarticulated aspiration for Ruth and for Boaz as redeemer, one that precludes Ruth's being taken off by one of his young men.

Ruth adheres to her mother-in-law's advice—and to Boaz's earlier injunction. In the book's fourth and final use of the verb *davaq*, she "cleaves" to Boaz's *young maidens* and she gleans with them to the end of both the barley and the wheat harvest. Nothing exciting happens—yet. Ruth continues to dwell quite happily with her mother-in-law. But about Naomi the text preserves silence—because Naomi as yet has nothing to say, not to Ruth and not to the reader. As with her reaction to Ruth's great speech, Naomi's silence here should not be taken for acquiescence or weakness. As Act Two comes to an end, Naomi, patient and prudent, keeps her own counsel and continues to bide her time.

Matchmaking

After Boaz's highly—overly—solicitous gestures toward Ruth on their first meeting in the fields, Naomi was curious to see what if anything he might do next. Would he at last make a visit to pay his respects—if only to see Ruth again, away from the fields? Had she not found favor in his eyes, in more ways than one? Had he not praised her virtue to the skies? Time passes. Nothing happens. Boaz neither calls nor approaches Ruth again in the fields. He remains aloof. Why?

Naomi considers to herself some plausible explanations. Had he extended himself toward Ruth that one time in order to make amends for his prior neglect of *her*, but without any further interest in Ruth herself? Or, more likely, had he in fact been interested in Ruth but afterward became reticent and shy? Why was he not fulfilling his duty as a kinsman-redeemer? Was he too much of a gentleman to force his older man's attentions on a young and still grieving widow? Was he concerned that she, being young, would refuse his overtures? Did he regard her Moabite origins as foreclosing any pursuit of her for marriage? If, as traditional commentators suggest, Boaz was himself a recent widower, that alone might explain his reluctance to approach Ruth.

Yet Naomi suspects that there may be another (or additional) explanation for Boaz's failure to act: yes, he is interested, but there is a kinsman closer than he, holding a prior claim as redeemer, and Boaz is reluctant to lose Ruth to anyone else. If this is the problem, how to solve it? Naomi continues to wait patiently for an opportune moment to find out what's what with Boaz. It comes soon enough, when urgent necessity and favorable circumstances coincide.

We have arrived at Act Three. The harvesting complete, but with still no movement from Boaz, Naomi recognizes that Ruth will not again—until the next harvest—have easy opportunity to be in his presence. Yet, as Naomi also recognizes, the celebratory feasting after the grain has been winnowed (please note: Naomi has

her ear to the ground) provides a golden opportunity
to bring Ruth to Boaz's attention, this time not as an
impoverished handmaid gleaning in his fields but as an
attractive woman equal to him in merit. Naomi seizes
on this last—and also best—chance to get Ruth married well. Initiative must lie with Ruth. Ruth must lie
with Boaz. Boaz must then rise to the occasion.

To start the ball rolling, Naomi, as director of the
drama, must first inspire Ruth to act on her own behalf.
This is the purpose of Naomi's speech that follows
immediately as the opening words in the book's third
chapter. It constitutes in essence her long-awaited reply
to her daughter-in-law's great speech to *her*. After pre-
senting the whole text, we'll read it line by line as in a
living conversation, pausing after each sentence to consider what Ruth might be thinking as she hears it.

> And [or, better, "But"] said to her Naomi her mother-
> in-law: "My daughter (*biti*), shall I not seek rest (*mano-
> ach*) for you, that it may be well with you? And now,
> is [there] not Boaz our kinsman (*moda'etanu*), with
> whose maidens you were? Behold him (*hinneh hu'*),
> he winnows barley in the threshing floor—tonight.
> Wash yourself therefore, and anoint yourself, and
> put your gown upon you, and get you down to the
> threshing floor; but make yourself not known to the
> man until he shall have done eating and drinking.
> And it shall be, when he lies down, that you shall
> mark the place where he shall lie, and you shall go
> in, and uncover his feet, and lay you down; and he
> will tell you what you shall do." And she said to her:
> "All that you say [to me] I will do." (3:1–5)

The first step is to get Ruth to think (again) about marriage. Ruth, we recall, had chosen lifelong friendship with Naomi over the prospect of remarriage back in Moab. She had sworn never to be separated from Naomi, until death do them part. In that spirit, Ruth still seems perfectly content to dwell with her and to live hand to mouth by gleaning. But the arduous experience in the field may have opened her to an alternative. Thus hopes Naomi.

Naomi begins by addressing Ruth not as mother-in-law but as mother: "My daughter." The tender invocation bespeaks not only greater intimacy but also solicitous concern, the concern of an aging mother for her unprotected daughter: You, my child, may not have given this a thought, but I, being old, must think about your future. Will you not indulge my concern for your wellbeing? Please listen and consider. After "My daughter"—in Hebrew, the endearing single word, *biti*—Ruth is all ears.

Naomi delicately puts the rhetorical question: should I not—as your "mother"—seek for you, my daughter, a condition of rest and security, that your life may become better? Naomi uses again the pregnant word *manoach*, translated "rest," that she had previously invoked when she urged Ruth and Orpah to return to Moab: "The Lord grant you that you may find rest, each of you in the house of her husband" (1:9). But whereas she had previously used the feminine form, *menuchah*, here she uses the masculine, *manoach*, which the medieval commentator Ibn Ezra understands to mean "husband." In Naomi's understanding of the world, dwelling even with a loving and virtuous mother-in-law (or "mother") is no home for a grown woman. She will have no security and she will have no rest—her inner restlessness will not cease—until she marries and, ultimately, until she gives birth.[23]

About Ruth's reaction to Naomi's opening question we can only speculate, as she keeps silent. Is she annoyed? What does Naomi want from me, she may be wondering? We now have a source of food, yet she wants me to leave? I recently lost a husband, why must I think of replacing him? Have I not vowed to abide with her, forever? Is my companionship not sufficient for her, or hers for me? Why is she pushing me out? Or, more likely, is Ruth pleased or, if not pleased, then at least neutral, open to hearing what Naomi has in mind? Our life is not easy. Naomi is wise and good and seeks my wellbeing. Let's see what she has to say.

Having obtained Ruth's attention with her opening question but not waiting for her to answer, Naomi delicately adds another leading question: Consider, please. Is there not this man Boaz, our kinsman? You know, the one with whose maidens you were working? Behold him. He will be winnowing barley on the threshing floor—tonight! (Again, note how well-informed Naomi has made herself.) Having put marriage before her, Naomi now puts Boaz before Ruth's mind as the prospective husband.

Ruth again keeps silence and does not answer. We can only imagine that the possibility does not displease her: Boaz is a prosperous landowner and a leader of the community. He has been most kind and gracious toward me, albeit on only that one occasion. Never mind that he is older. He is a man for windy weather. Indeed, with him I—and Naomi—would have a home in this community, perhaps even a place in its history. On such grounds, Ruth seems more than willing to hear Naomi's forthcoming advice on how to advance this match and how to take advantage of the opportunity that knocks, tonight, on the threshing floor.

Without waiting for Ruth to answer, Naomi gives Ruth the plan intended to land Boaz as her husband. The words of the instructions are more or less clear, even if their meaning is not. Bathed, anointed, and finely clad, she is to go to the threshing floor for the festivities that attend the conclusion of the day of winnowing. She is to hold herself apart from Boaz until he has had his fill of food and drink. Carefully noticing where he lies down for the night, Ruth is to enter his spot after he is asleep, where she must "uncover his feet" and lie down beside him. Boaz, says Naomi, will then tell her what she should do.

What exactly is Naomi directing Ruth to do? No surprise, the commentators disagree. As is so often the case, what readers see in a story reflects both who *they* are and especially what they want to see. To us, as uncommitted readers, on first glance it looks for all the world as if Naomi is counseling seduction: Ruth is to appear perfumed and in her finery. She is to meet Boaz not as one of the maids in his field but as her beautified self, and as his equal. She is not to meet him wide-awake in broad daylight but under cover of darkness—indeed, under the covers; she will be in his bed when he awakes in the middle of the night. The rest Naomi is content to leave to Ruth's imagination—and Boaz's.

The situation is certainly sexually charged. But what Ruth is to do there depends especially on how she understands Naomi's order to "uncover his feet." Should she take it literally, she will expose his feet—and perhaps, symbolically, the fact of his having had "cold feet" in her direction—and throw herself upon them as a suppliant, hoping he will recognize the gesture and know what should be done. Should she, however, take it euphemistically—and there is ample biblical precedent for using "feet" or "legs" as a euphemism for the male genitalia—she will uncover his sexual nakedness and offer herself to him for the night, hoping for more. Readers with a long biblical memory will remember that, in Genesis, the eponymous founder of Moab was conceived when Lot's elder daughter seduced her father under cover of darkness, after she had made him drunk with wine. On this reading, Ruth is being invited to be true to her origins, to play Lot's daughter.

As for readers who remember the story of Judah and Tamar, they may be tempted to see that Ruth is also being asked to imitate Tamar, who placed herself sexually in Judah's path (at the end of the sheep shearing) after he had refused to allow his youngest son to fulfill the levirate duty as he had promised her. Boaz, we have noted earlier, springs from that incestuous union. And like Judah, Boaz has been tardy in playing the role of the redeemer. Yes, there are crucial differences: Ruth is to present herself not disguised like Tamar as a harlot, but adorned as herself. And Boaz, unlike Judah, is supposed to *recognize* her and to *tell* her what is to be done. But the echo of Tamar's seduction of Judah makes us wonder whether the similarities are not more significant than the differences.

Most traditional commentators will have none of this. They insist that the encounter to which Naomi sent Ruth was intended to be—and was in fact—entirely chaste. Naomi and Ruth are dignified and moral women who cannot even imagine playing the harlot, and Boaz, everyone knows, is a God-fearing man. Naomi's goal, they rightly remind us, is not a one-night stand but marriage and redemption. But in making this case, they have to exert their moral ingenuity and moral authority to overcome what they themselves recognize as the text's risqué appearance. Rashi, for example (1040–1105), says that Ruth, being concerned that going all dolled up to the threshing floor would make her look like a prostitute, actually waited to dress up until she arrived. Forestalling any possible euphemistic reading of "feet," Ralbag (Gersonides, 1288–1344) says that it signifies "the place where the feet are." Another commentator says that Naomi, assured through long trial of the good behavior and firm chasteness of her daughter-in-law, and persuaded of the nobility and religious gravity of Boaz, would naturally have regarded as safe a design that for others would have been perilous. Notwithstanding these cleansing remarks, the Midrash in *Ruth Rabbah*, acknowledging the eroticism of the encounter, claims that Boaz had to exercise greater sexual restraint toward Ruth than did Joseph when he was propositioned by Potiphar's wife.

For now, we will refrain from choosing sides and keep an open mind. Hoping the situation will clarify itself, we read on.

A Night on the Threshing Floor

What Ruth herself understood of Naomi's instructions we are not told. But she asks no questions and raises no objections. Like the Children of Israel presented with the Lord's covenant before Mount Sinai (Exodus 19:7), she does not hesitate to give her complete assent: "All that you say, I will do." Ruth proceeds immediately to carry out the plan.

> And she went down to the threshing floor, and did according to all that her mother-in-law had ordered her. And when Boaz had eaten and drunk, and his heart (*lev*) was merry, he went to lie down at the end of the heap of corn; and she came softly (or "secretly"; *vallat*, "with *lat*," "secrecy"), and uncovered his feet, and laid her down. (3:6–7)

Three things deserve comment.

First, some commentators, Rashi among them, make much of the fact that the text first says that she went down to the threshing floor and only then reports that she did all that Naomi had commanded.[24] Ruth is following the spirit, not the letter, of Naomi's orders; she uses her initiative to adapt the order of her deeds to the circumstances. In a moment, we will see Ruth's inventiveness in its full glory.

Second, although Boaz ate and drank, there is no suggestion of excess. Unlike Noah and Lot, the first famous biblical drinkers, there is no mention of drunkenness. Boaz's "heart was merry," not, as is said of King Ahashuerus in the Book of Esther, "merry with wine." When Ruth arrives, Boaz is sleeping, but he is not "sleeping it off." She will take advantage of his good cheer and contentment but not, as did Lot's elder daughter (and Moab's mother), of his drunkenness: a condition that she herself had induced in order to lie with him safely.

Third, the description of Ruth's arrival, as usually translated, seems innocent enough. She comes softly, in secret, uncovers his feet, and lays herself down in that place. Still, there are small echoes of less innocent episodes. The word translated "softly," *lat*, is used only five more times in the Bible, none of them innocent.[25] Moreover, the verbs, "she came . . . she laid her down (*vatavo' . . . vatishkav*)" are identical to the verbs used for Lot's elder daughter: "and she came (*vatavo'*), the first-born, and she laid her down (*vatishkav*) with her father" (Genesis 19:33). One might even suspect a near pun, of "*lat*," and Lot (*lot*).

In our opinion, however, these echoes serve rather to call attention to crucial differences: Ruth came with *lat*, but not with witchcraft, and she laid herself down at Boaz's feet; by contrast, Lot's daughter lay down *with her father*, whom she had made so drunk that "he knew not when she lay down, nor when she arose" (Genesis 19:33). Ruth, the Moabitess, is *not* repeating the illicit and unsavory practice that give birth to her Moabite ancestor. On the contrary, although making herself sexually available she practices full self-command, her thoughts fixed on the elevated prospect before her. Moreover, Boaz, who awakens without confusion or hangover, is neither a Lot nor a Judah. He almost immediately grasps the full meaning of the situation, and everything he does is more than honorable.

And it happened (*vayehi*) at midnight, that the man
was startled (*vayyecherad*; [usually rendered "trem-
bled"]), and turned himself over; and, behold, a
woman lay at his feet. And he said: "Who are you
(*mi 'at*)?" And she answered: "I am Ruth your maidservant (*'amathekha*); spread therefore your skirt (or
"cloak" or "wing"; *kanaf*) over your maidservant
(*'amathekha*); for you are a kinsman-redeemer
(*go'el*)." (3:8–9)

In the middle of the night, Boaz is startled out of
sleep—a bad dream? a prophecy?—and even more
startled by what he finds when he turns himself over
(around): a woman is lying at his feet. (It seems that
Ruth understood "feet" literally; she appears as a suppliant.) Yet although he is surprised, he keeps his cool.
He does not challenge her presence; he asks only for
her identity. What kind of woman would lie down at
my feet, and, moreover, not make herself known in any
way? "Who are you?"

This simple question, seeking identity, can be answered at many levels, from the more superficial to the
more profound: What is your name? Are you a harlot,
or not? What is your intention, aspiration, and purpose?
Declare yourself! Beneath these concrete and obvious
concerns, Boaz's question also addresses the deep mystery of the human person, an uncanny mixture of the
familiar and the strange—a universal conundrum vivified here by the fact of Ruth's foreignness. We listen
with Boaz, and with bated breath, for Ruth's answer.

Boaz may not be surprised by the name he hears, but
he—and we—could not have expected what Ruth says

next, or even *that* she makes bold to speak. Naomi had told Ruth that Boaz would tell *her* what to do, but it is Ruth who gives the orders. For the first and only time in the Book, Ruth utters her own name. And she immediately conveys the truth of her being in what she says next. This is the moment at which we discover why the book is named for Ruth.

Ruth begins humbly: I am Ruth, your maidservant[26]—a lowly individual, seeking your protection. But what follows is hardly humble. Ruth commands Boaz to spread his skirt (or "wing"; *kanaf*) over her and, moreover, tells him *why* he should do so: "because you are a redeemer (*go'el*)." You have a responsibility toward Naomi and me, which I have come here to get you to fulfill—and I am making it graphically clear how you might do it. Remember, Boaz, how you blessed me and asked the Lord to recompense me? Remember how you asked that I be rewarded for having sought refuge under the protecting wings (*kanaf*) of the Lord God of Israel (2:12)? Well, I am now seeking refuge under *your* wings, as a means of making good on your blessing. I, your servant, am summoning you to do the Lord's work—by marrying me.

We readers—and no doubt Boaz—are astonished by the courage and clarity of Ruth's speech, which springs forth from the depths of her soul, uninstructed and unrehearsed. A mere ten Hebrew words, it is every bit as impressive as her great friendship speech to Naomi. Although at risk of rejection and loss of reputation, Ruth has read Boaz's character perfectly. Her speech, seizing on his own words to exhort him to fulfill his role as a redeemer in Israel, finds its mark. "What kind of mar-

vel of intelligence and character . . . to know that these
words ('spread your wings') were just the ones to say to
make the impossible possible?"[27]

Boaz rises to the occasion. He gives prompt and direct
response to Ruth's three-part statement in a three-part
answer of his own, the epitome of delicacy and grace.

> And he said: "Blessed be you of the Lord, my
> daughter; you have shown more *chesed* ("loyal devo-
> tion" or " gracious kindness") in the end than at
> the beginning, inasmuch as you did not follow
> the young men, whether poor or rich. And now,
> my daughter, fear not; I will do to you all that you
> say; for all the men in the gate of my people know
> that you are a virtuous woman ("woman of valor";
> *'esheth chayil*). And now, surely it is true that I am a
> redeemer (*go'el*); but there is also a redeemer (*go'el*)
> nearer than I. Tarry this night, and it shall be in
> the morning, that if he will redeem you (*yig'alekh*),
> good, he will redeem. But if he does not wish to
> redeem you (*lega'olekh*), then I myself will redeem
> you (*ug'altikh*), as the Lord lives! Lie down until the
> morning." (3:10–13)

First, Boaz answers Ruth's humble "your maidservant" with his affectionate "my daughter." Though this
"paternal" term of endearment might be seen as cast-
ing a slight shadow over his acceptance of her implicit
proposal of marriage, and though the tacit allusion to
incest in both their ancestries may be intentional, he
neither takes advantage of her nor castigates her for her

forwardness. Deeply touched, he again calls down the Lord's blessing upon her, this time for her new act of loyal devotion (or "gracious kindness"; *chesed*) *to him*, greater than she showed in leaving home and homeland to cleave to Naomi. She has thrown herself at his feet, placing herself in a compromising position and at risk of being taken for a loose woman, all to indicate that she has kindly chosen him as her intended, in preference to many younger men. She offers to save him from a lonely old age, an offer that Boaz (especially if, as some have it, a widower) might feel most profoundly; she promises now to cleave only to him. More precisely, despite her youth and despite her foreign origins, she has graced him with a chance to cleave *to her* and to perform the obligation of redeemer.

Boaz's praise of Ruth's *chesed*—the book's third (and last) use of the term and the only one ascribed to a human being—invites us here to probe more deeply the nature of this virtue and its contagious effects. For *chesed* is not just a mindless passion, a soft feeling of lovingkindness, an indiscriminately aroused expression of a warm heart. Like all virtues of character, *chesed* is a grown-together-ness of good heart and keen mind. It involves moral perception, an intuitive awareness of some intrinsic good in others—beyond wealth or status, birth or nationality—that elicits the overt responses of kindness and devotion, grace and loyalty. Ruth has perceived that Boaz is a virtuous and God-fearing man, and she responds by singling him out for gracious kindness. Vindicating the praise of him that is implicit in her word and deed ("spread your wing . . . you are a redeemer," "lay at his feet"), Boaz recognizes her virtue and responds with gracious words and noble deeds of his own.

Second ("And now"), Boaz reassures Ruth that her *chesed* toward him will be reciprocated. He lets her know that he has understood her gesture and the meaning of her request to "spread [his] wing (or "skirt" or "cloak"; *kanaf*) over [his] handmaid." Not to worry, Ruth, and do not fear. "All that you say, I will do [for you]"—Ruth's very words in response to Naomi's strategic instructions (3:5): your wish is my command. Why? Because, says Boaz, again "legislating" in advance for the community, *everyone* knows that you are a virtuous woman—which is to say, not a seducing and licentious Moabitess—and a worthy match for a virtuous Israelite. Tacitly echoing his ancestor Judah's confession regarding Tamar as "more righteous" than he, Boaz, introduced by the text as *'ish gibor chayil*, "a mighty man of valor," confesses to having been "conquered"—smitten—by a virtuous "woman of valor" (*'esheth chayil*).[28]

Finally ("And now"), Boaz reveals a difficulty, one that may have partly accounted for his prior reticence and neglect. Yes, it is true, I am indeed your kinsman-redeemer (*go'el*); but (alas) "there is another redeemer who is nearer than I." If Ruth will but spend the night, Boaz promises to deal with this complication the very next morning. He will force the issue: either the nearer kinsman will promptly agree to accept the role of redeemer or, should he refuse, Boaz—swearing an oath!—promises that he will do so himself. Meanwhile, says he to Ruth, lie down and sleep until the morning. Peacefully. Chastely. As the Lord lives, I will do right by you—tomorrow, and also tonight and hereafter.

Ruth does as Boaz directs:

> And she lay at his feet until the morning; and she
> rose up before one could discern another. For he
> said [likely to himself]: "Let it not be known that
> the woman came to the threshing floor." And he
> said: "Bring the mantle that is upon you, and hold
> it"; and she held it; and he measured six measures of
> barley (*shesh se'orim*; literally, "six barleys"), and laid
> it on her; and he went into the city. (3:14–15)

Ruth spends the night with Boaz (merely at his feet),
but leaves before dawn. No one will recognize her; no
one will know that she had been there; no one will be
able to suspect her of indecency. But before she leaves,
Boaz makes her a sizable present of barley from the day's
winnowing—at once a bequest to meet her needs, a gift
of gratitude for her loyal devotion, a token of his pledge
to redeem her, an engagement present or bride-price,
and a symbol of fertility and fruitfulness in anticipation
of the redemptive fertility and fruitfulness that Ruth is
seeking from her redeemer. As he lays the barley upon
her shoulder (or head), Boaz himself heads for the city to
carry out his promise.

Reporting to Naomi

Ruth arrives back home, bearing barley. Naomi, no
doubt after a restless but eager night, is up and waiting
for her.

> And when she came to her mother-in-law, she
> [Naomi] said: "Who are you, my daughter (*mi 'at*

biti)?" And she told her all that the man had done to her. And she said: "These six measures of barley gave he me; for he said to me: 'Go not empty (*reqam*) to your mother-in-law.'" Then said she [Naomi]: "Sit still, my daughter, until you know how the matter will fall; for the man will not rest (*lo' yishqot*) until he have finished the thing this day." (3:16–18)

On her arrival, Ruth is again confronted—for the second time in but a few hours—with the need to identify herself: "Who are you—my daughter (*mi 'at, biti*)?" Boaz had asked, wondering what sort of woman had thrown herself at his feet, and was surprised and delighted to know that this was no harlot but a woman of *chesed* seeking a redemptive marriage. Naomi asks not because she has failed to recognize Ruth—she calls her "my daughter"—but because she wants to know whether she be married or not; for a marriage can be established though an act of sexual concourse. But, as Ruth informs Naomi, she is not yet married. Indeed, she tells her the whole story of the night on the threshing floor, and especially all the things that Boaz had said and done in her direction. She concludes by explaining her possession of the barley: Boaz, Ruth says, wanted her to "go not empty to your mother-in-law."

Naomi immediately understands how things stand. No, Ruth is not yet married. But she soon will be. Boaz will see to it, and straightaway. The gift of the barley to Ruth, Naomi sees, is intended also as a sign and pledge for *her*: Boaz has indeed grasped the larger meaning of Ruth's appeal at his feet. He has been called to redeem not only Ruth but also Naomi, and to raise up an heir also to Naomi, that her son Mahlon should not disappear without a trace. The clue is the reprise of the term "empty." When Naomi had returned from Moab, she had complained, "I went out full, but the Lord has brought me back empty (*reqam*)"—destitute and childless. Boaz wants Naomi to know that she will soon be empty no longer.

Armed with this understanding, Naomi is able to counsel Ruth on what to expect. Be patient. Sit tight. The man will be true to his word. Boaz will take care of everything, today. As the curtain descends on Act Three, rising hope has displaced despair.

Boaz, Redeemer

Boaz wastes no time in fulfilling his promise. His goal is simple: to marry Ruth. But success will require prudence, not to say cunning. He must get the other kinsman to relinquish his prior claim. He must also get the community to accept this (forbidden) marriage. Early the next morning, with plan in mind, he heads for the gathering place before the city gate, where public business is conducted and legal cases are heard, and he settles in to await the arrival of the other kinsman-redeemer. Throughout this entire episode, Boaz will act with energy, dispatch, and confident authority, as befits a man of his standing (*'ish gibor chayil*), character, and determined purpose.

> Now Boaz went up to the gate, and he sat himself down (*vayyeshev*) there; and, behold (*hinneh*), the near-kinsman ("redeemer," *go'el*) of whom Boaz

spoke came by; to whom he said: "Ho, 'So-and-
So' (*peloni 'almoni*; literally, "such-a-one" or "such-
and-such")! Turn aside, sit down here." And he
turned aside, and he sat down (*vayyeshev*). And he
[Boaz] took ten men of the elders of the city—and
he said: "Sit you down here." And they sat down
(*vayyeshvu*). (4:1–2)

Arriving early and seated before the gate, Boaz does
not have long to wait. "Behold": the man he is seeking
suddenly appears. This the second (and last) time in the
book that the right person arrives at just the right moment. The first appearance of Boaz was also heralded by
the suggestive word "Behold" (*hinneh*; 2:4): two remarkable arrivals, both advancing the remarriage of Ruth.
Coincidence? Luck? Destiny? Providence?[29]

Boaz orders the man to sit; the man sits. Boaz gath-
ers a quorum of city elders hanging around the gate and
orders them to sit as well. The elders sit. To no one does
Boaz say "please": he has charismatic and commanding authority. The elders have been summoned to witness a private negotiation but one having, little do they
know, important consequences for the whole community, indeed, for the entire Jewish people.

Who is the man? We are not told. Because he is said
to be a kinsman nearer to Elimelech than Boaz, commentators have suggested—but without textual evidence—that he is Elimelech's brother (and Mahlon's
uncle) or maybe even Boaz's older brother. In our view,
neither is likely. More striking than the missing identi-
fication of the other kinsman's relationship to Elimelech
is the absence of his name. Boaz, who obviously knows

this relative, addresses him strangely. *Peloni 'almoni*—translated here as "So-and-So," but renderable also as "Joe Blow," "John Doe," or "Mac"—is not a proper name but a deliberately anonymous designation. How to explain this obtrusive namelessness?

In general, a character may go unnamed because he or his identity is unimportant: no one in particular, anyone at all. A nameless man may also represent a type: an everyman, an average guy, a fill-in-the-blank "John Doe." Alternatively, a character may be unnamed because he has done nothing to earn being mentioned or, worse, because he has done something worth hiding. He deserves *not* to be remembered; his identity has been covered over in shame. His name, we are meant to think, has been "erased."

Several of these reasons, we will soon see, apply in the present situation. Although we cannot know Boaz's reasons, his failure to address the man by name turns out to be prophetic. So-and-So will reveal himself to be an average fellow, in contrast to whom the text can display the superior virtue of Boaz. (In this respect, he functions like Orpah in the opening chapter: an average woman who at first gestures in a lofty direction but in the end makes an average person's choice; her presence and choice set off the rare and superior virtue of Ruth.) In addition, the text will refuse to embarrass him by recording his name. He will remain forever a forgotten man mainly because he deserves, in his shame, not to be known. Indeed, his anonymity turns out to be the perfect "retribution" for his refusal to ensure "that the *name* of the dead not be cut off from among his brethren" (4:10; emphasis added).

The witnesses assembled, Boaz informs his kinsman of the purpose of the meeting: the redemption of land.

> And he said to the redeemer (*go'el*): "A parcel of land (*chelqath hassadeh*) that was our brother Elimelech's (*le'achinu le'elimelekh*), Naomi is selling (*makhrah*; from *makhar*, "sell")—[Naomi] the one returning (*hashavah*, from *shuv*) out of the field of Moab.[30] So I, I resolved to let you know [about this], saying: 'Buy it before them that sit here, and before the elders of my people. If you will redeem it, redeem it; but if he will not redeem it, tell me, that I may know; for there is none to redeem it beside you; and I am after you.'" And he [So-and-So] said: "I, I will redeem it." (4:3–4)

Boaz opens by dangling land in front of the man, land that belonged to "our brother Elimelech": That land, you will be pleased to know, is now for sale; Naomi has determined to sell it. Shifting his attention from the man to the seated witnesses and back to the man again—"if *you* will"; "if *he* will not"; "beside *you*" and "I am after *you*"—Boaz creates a sense of urgency for decision: redeem the land now, or publicly surrender your claim. Only we two can do this and keep it in the family, you or I.

As we await So-and-So's response, we are filled with wonder at Boaz's confident assertion of Naomi's intention to sell the land. How did he learn about it, seeing as he has yet to speak with Naomi? (In our hearing, he never does.) Was this an inference drawn from Ruth's reminding him—last night, under the covers—that he was her *go'el*, her "kinsman redeemer"? We marvel again at Boaz's ingenuity and "legislating" authority.[31]

So-and-So does not hesitate: "I, I will redeem it." And, he must be thinking, why not? I get to enlarge my family estate; I provide financial help to Naomi; I prevent my kinsman Elimelech's land from going to a stranger.

Not so fast, *peloni 'almoni*. Boaz, as if reading a contract's fine print, promptly shows So-and-So that he incompletely understands what it means to redeem a portion of the Promised Land.

> Then said Boaz: "On the day you buy the field from the hand of Naomi, you have also bought ("accepted") Ruth the Moabitess, the wife of the dead (*'esheth hammeth*)—to raise up the name of the dead (*shem hammeth*) upon his inheritance (*nachalatho*)." (4:5)

Revealing additional information that he hopes will discourage So-and-So, Boaz now makes explicit the full meaning of redeeming the land. The land, he insists, automatically comes with the widow of its late owner, meaning by the latter not Elimelech but Elimelech's son Mahlon—thus for the first time dramatically introducing both Mahlon and Ruth into a completely changed picture. The land is not free-floating real estate; each portion is an allocated and permanent share in the Promised Land. It belongs to a family, and the family belongs to it. In the present case, Elimelech's land, whether sold earlier or not, properly belongs only with his heirs. But because his heirs are also dead, their name can be kept "upright" in Israel only by arranging for their land to stay in the family, to be inherited by a son raised to them for this purpose. Doing so requires marrying the widow Ruth—whom, please note, Boaz pointedly refers to as "the Moabitess, the wife of the dead"—and providing her a son who can lift up the name of his dead father along with his inheritance.

We marvel at Boaz's brilliant rhetorical feat. He pulls Ruth, widow of Elimelech's heir, out of his hat and into a marital picture that he paints most unattractively: not only Ruth, but Ruth the Moabitess; not only Ruth the Moabitess, but Ruth the wife of the dead; not only Ruth the wife of the dead, but one whom he must marry—why? to raise up the name of the dead ex-husband upon his land. Intuiting the deep connection between the commandments of *yibbum* (levirate marriage) and *ge'ulah* (land redemption), Boaz asserts here—*de novo*—that a levirate-like obligation is attached to this sale of land.

Although the linkage of these two commandments becomes a later obligation in Jewish law, it has no explicit biblical foundation. It is, rather, of rabbinic origin. But Boaz, once again "legislating" the practice of *chesed*, anticipates the rabbis' later insight: redeeming land for which there is no heir is but a hollow redemption. The family's ongoing attachment to the land, like the perpetuation of God's Way, requires procreation.[32]

Equally bold, Boaz pronounces the Moabite widow eligible for marriage in Bethlehem, in effect annulling the Mosaic prohibition of any kind of intercourse with the Moabites and legislating her into the community—acts displaying his great *chesed* and his impressive authority. The primary target of Boaz's remarks is *peloni 'almoni*, to get him to reconsider. But he is at the same time educating the civic elders to accept Ruth into the community and to look favorably on what he hopes will be his own impending marriage.

The extra obligations are too much for So-and-So. He panics and changes his mind.

> And the near kinsman said: "I cannot redeem it for myself, lest I ruin (*'ashchith*) my own inheritance (*nachalathi*); take you my right of redemption on yourself; for I cannot redeem it." (4:6)

Why does So-and-So change his mind? Why does he refuse to redeem the land, as he had originally agreed to do? What kind of "ruining" of his inheritance does he fear?

Like any average human being, So-and-So thinks mainly of himself and concerns himself with his advantage. Extra land is an obvious gain; an obligatory marriage, not so much. It is not only that he is already married—which, although we are not told, he very likely is—and therefore eager to avoid family rivalries. It is not only that he would have the burden and expense of fathering and raising a child who would count as someone else's and who would someday inherit the redeemed land he was hoping to deliver to his own children. It is, we suspect, mainly that he must marry a Moabitess, a woman from the despised and forbidden enemy people and, moreover, an ominous risk, "the wife of the dead." Although So-and-So surely knew of Ruth's existence and of her widowed condition, it never occurred to him that she, as an outsider, was eligible for such levirate-like remarriage; after all, there was Moses' injunction against Moabites entering into the congregation of Israel. Marrying Ruth and fathering children by her, thinks So-

and-So, will lower his social standing, jeopardize family harmony, and corrupt the inheritance he will leave his own children. I really can't afford to do this, Boaz. You may have the honor.

Boaz's strategy has worked. So-and-So takes a pass, leaving the field to him. We readers are delighted at this turn of events. Having borne witness against himself, So-and-So has not only proved himself unworthy of Ruth; he has also earned the erasure of his name.

Yet before we rush to convict him, we should consider whether we—average people ourselves—would have chosen differently: how many of us would gladly marry, only out of a putative moral responsibility, the foreign-born widowed wife (from an enemy nation) of a deceased second cousin whom we hadn't seen in ten years, to sire and rear a son that will be his, not ours? So-and-So is not embarrassed by his choice. We doubt that he minds not having his name recorded for posterity. Moreover, the text does not condemn him for his decision, in contrast to the Torah's condemnation (see Deuteronomy 25:5–10) of the man who refuses to raise up a name in Israel for his deceased *brother*. Heroic choices are never obligatory, and they will not be embraced by the world's many So-and-Sos—especially when, unlike Boaz, they lack personal appreciation of and desire for the widow herself.

All that remains is for the deal to be ratified. And so it was.

> Now this was the custom in former time in Israel
> concerning redeeming and concerning exchanging,

> to confirm all things: a man drew off his shoe, and
> gave it to his neighbor; and this was the attestation
> in Israel. So the near kinsman said unto Boaz: "Buy
> it for yourself." And he drew off his shoe. (4:7–8)

In an unusual backward reference to a "former time
in Israel," the voice of the text distances itself, for the
first time since its opening sentence ("in the days of the
judging of judges") from the story it is narrating—presumably to call attention to a custom no longer in use.
(At the end, the voice of the text will make a forward
reference to the time of King David.) The drawing-off
of one's shoe was, not only in ancient Israel but also in
other places, a symbolic act of legal transfer: a represen-
tation of a deed of sale.

Why a shoe? All sorts of suggestions have been offered. The practical-minded Abraham Ibn Ezra focuses
on the ready availability of shoes for such exchanges.
More spiritualizing commentators hold that the removal
of the shoe acknowledges both the holiness of all human
agreements and the truthfulness of the human agent, by
removing artifice from the way a man treads the earth
and the holy land. (Moses at the burning bush was told
by God to remove his shoes since he stood on sacred
ground.) Ambiguity also attends the matter of *whose*
shoe was removed, with rabbinic scholars taking opposite sides. The syntax seems to favor the view that the
shoe was So-and-So's, given as a sign that he is ceding
his right of redemption. It is thus surely meant to remind us of the *chalitsah* ceremony, discussed earlier, that
humiliates the man who refuses to perform levirate marriage with his brother's widow. By this echoing, some

opprobrium falls also on So-and-So even though he has
not violated any extant commandment. Yet the ambiguous wording may also imply that, when told by the kinsman to "Buy it for yourself," it is Boaz who responds
promptly with his own shoe.

But there is nothing ambiguous in what happens
next, as Boaz proudly declares the meaning of the trans-
action, not only before the elders but also before all who
are present at the gate:

> And Boaz said unto the elders, and unto all the peo-
> ple: "You are witnesses this day (*'edim 'atem hayyom*),
> that I have bought (*qanithi*) all that was Elim-
> elech's, and all that was Chilion's and Mahlon's, of
> the hand of Naomi. Moreover Ruth the Moabitess,
> the wife of Mahlon, have I purchased (*qanithi*) to
> be my wife, to raise up the name of the dead upon
> his inheritance, that the name of the dead be not
> cut off from among his brethren, and from the gate
> of his place; you are witnesses this day (*'edim 'atem
> hayyom*)." (4:9–10)

Boaz calls upon everyone to witness that he has properly purchased from Naomi the right to the complete
estates—note that he does not here emphasize the *land*,
as he did with So-and-So—of Elimelech and of his two
sons. But for Boaz, the heart of the matter is a matter of
the heart. He wants everyone to acknowledge that he has
also "purchased" the right to marry Ruth. When pre-
senting the matter to So-and-So, Boaz had rubbed his
nose in her Moabite origins, suspecting (correctly) that
that fact might put him off; here, in claiming her for
himself, he subordinates those Moabite origins to Ruth's

being the wife—not the widow—of Mahlon (and not, as he called her to So-and-So, "the wife of the dead"). By force of his person and the example of his *chesed*, Boaz "legislates" for the community the conversion of Ruth from "despised other" and "wife of the dead" to "wife of one of our own" and "my intended."

Not only that. He will marry Ruth, he wants everyone to know, to put right the childlessness of her marriage to Mahlon. As both her and *his* redeemer, he intends to give Ruth children who will be reckoned as Mahlon's and who will thereby rescue his name from oblivion by possessing his share of the land and transmitting it untrammeled to his own descendants. By reclaiming land and siring descendants, redeeming both the living and the dead, Boaz will guarantee to Mahlon an enduring place among his brethren and his city.

Two large matters deserve comment. First, Boaz here completes the integration of Ruth into the Israelite community. As the wife of Mahlon, as the daughter-in-law (*kallah*) of Naomi, as the woman who left her homeland, her family, and her gods to cleave to Naomi, Ruth may have long felt herself to be an Israelite. But in the eyes of the community, she was still a Moabite, a person who could never be counted among the Children of Israel. Yet already on the day of their first meeting at the barley harvest, Boaz had magnanimously set aside Ruth's Moabite origins and, in front of his own workers, had treated her as a woman of valor. Her character and her deeds of *chesed*—and perhaps also his attraction to her—outweighed the accident of her birth, at least for purposes of granting her permission to glean and sharing a meal with her in public. Today, Boaz consummates that welcoming and transformative gesture not only by marrying her, but also by insisting that the community accept his way of regarding her. As we shall see, he succeeds completely.

The second matter has been a subject of debate: why does Boaz do all of this for Ruth and Naomi? Is he just doing his altruistic duty as a redeemer, moved by the example of Ruth's devotion to Naomi? Or is he also in love with Ruth, won over by her loveliness and grace—and by her tender nocturnal appearance and firm proposal? Commentators do not agree.

Boaz's declaration of his intent to marry Ruth, we grant, is hardly passionate. It is all about a *go'el's* disinterested performance of his duty. Indeed, Boaz speaks less about the living woman than about her departed husband. Ruth had once spoken of her devotion to Naomi in terms one uses only toward a spouse. Boaz speaks about Ruth as prospective spouse only in terms of devotion to her dead husband. Where, you might ask, is love in all of this?[33]

Do not be fooled. Boaz's public declaration to the community does not fully reveal his heart, which, gentleman that he is, he will not wear on his sleeve. The reason for the gathering, we should remember, is a strictly legal matter: to obtain the obligation/right of first redeemer for Naomi's family. But if So-and So has his mind on land and profit, the noble Boaz has his heart set on Ruth.

Boaz had witnessed and marveled at her grace and loyal devotion when first they met. But after excessive initial attentions, he kept his distance, refusing to take advantage of his wealth and status to entice this young widow to leave Naomi (who needed her companionship) and marry a too-much-older man, especially when So-and-So had a prior claim to her hand. But Ruth's conduct on the previous night had given him courage and resolve. More precisely, Ruth enabled him to overcome his reticence by revealing that *she* had fixed her affection and regard on *him*: Wonder of wonders, miracle of miracles, my feelings for her are reciprocated.

True, we see here none of the usual passionate signs of erotic love, but we cannot therefore conclude that they are absent. The nobility of Ruth and Boaz precludes public displays—or even protestations—of erotic longings. More important, theirs is not that kind of love story, as Alan Rubenstein has written:

> Panting, swooning, and infatuation might be the usual condition of men and women in the throes of erotic attraction, but time and again Boaz and Ruth are revealed as two exemplary human beings if not giants among mere men, comporting themselves with the dignity that suits their greatness. . . . If a love story requires focusing on the emotions of the would-be lovers and the tensions inherent in their unresolved longing for each other, then no, this is not a [romantic] love story. . . . But if a love story can be one that reaches its happy end by presenting the uplifting union in marriage and procreation of two excellent individuals who can be said uniquely to deserve each other, then this is a great love story indeed.[34]

Just so: it is love and loyal devotion, and not merely moral duty, that govern Boaz's final pledge to raise up

Mahlon's name upon his inheritance and to make sure
that his name is not cut off from among his people. The
deepest love is not a painful lack seeking satisfaction for
oneself, but a bountiful overflow seeking the good for
one's beloved, in generative acts both large and small. In
his loving desire to fill the void in Ruth's life, caused by
the death of Mahlon, Boaz gladly seeks to provide her
also with "his" child, a child that will, as a replacement
for them both, preserve her first love's name in Israel.

The Witnesses Rejoice

Boaz's speech to the elders and the other people at the
gate more than succeeds. Their response is remarkable.

> And all the people that were in the gate, and the
> elders, said: "We are witnesses. The Lord make the
> woman that is come into your house like Rachel
> and like Leah, which two did build the house of
> Israel; and do you nobly (*chayil*) in Ephrath, and be
> famous in Bethlehem; and let your house be like the
> house of Perez, whom Tamar bore unto Judah, of
> the seed which the Lord shall give you of this young
> woman." (4:11–12)

Erupting with enthusiasm, all the assembled—the
people even ahead of the elders—eagerly and unani-
mously bear witness to Boaz's proposed transactions. In
giving their hearty approval, they elevate their voices in
prophetic utterance, functioning like a Greek chorus—
but in a comedy, not a tragedy. They bespeak the text's
vision about the redemptive possibilities of procreation.

Picking up on Boaz's emphasis, the witnesses speak only about the woman; they say not a word about the redeemed land. How their attitude toward Ruth has changed! Although they do not utter her name, they welcome her fully into the community; they no longer care that she is—was—a Moabite. Most remarkably, they call forth upon her a grand and glorious blessing: that the Lord make her like the matriarchal sisters Rachel and Leah, the wives of Jacob/Israel who gave birth to his twelve sons, who in turn gave rise to the Israelite nation. Thanks to Boaz's bold proposal of marriage, Ruth's standing in the eyes of the community has risen from lowly Moabite outsider to peer of the matriarchs. God willing, she, too, will build up the nation of Israel—in her case, a growth that will be not in numbers but in greatness.

(Notably, the witnesses have overlooked the unseemly and bitter rivalry between Rachel and Leah, no doubt because of its prolific generative result. As we shall see, the same emphasis on procreation may explain the text's "forgetfulness" of ancient incest in the lines of both Ruth and Boaz.)

The "chorus" has not finished. It also has words for Boaz. The people and elders call down blessings of nobility and fame upon him, and conclude with a most astonishing prayer. Speaking as if they had each just read the book of Genesis, they conjure up events that occurred seven generations ago to bless the house of Boaz: may his house prosper from the offspring that the Lord will give him of his young bride, the way the house of Perez prospered after Tamar bore him for Judah.

How the people in the gate were—was it divinely?—inspired to think of Perez (and Judah and Tamar) is, to say the least, a mystery. But there can be little doubt that they are speaking for the biblical author. What, then, are they saying? They are offering an implicit teaching about the intrinsic meaning of marriage and procreation and their connection with the community. To understand this more fully, we must look again at the story in Genesis of Judah and Tamar, comparing it with our present tale.

Boaz chooses freely to marry the widow Ruth and to redeem—through siring her child—the name of her late husband. By contrast, Judah, Boaz's ancestor, had initially thwarted such redemption. Fearing for his youngest son's life, he kept him from marrying his widowed daughter-in-law and redeeming the name of her dead husband. It was Tamar, playing the harlot, who induced her father-in-law to raise up seed to his eldest son, thus preventing him from disappearing without a trace. Although theirs was an incestuous union that would later be condemned at Sinai, Tamar's deed taught Judah the future-affirming and community-preserving meaning of marriage. By his very birth and being, Perez—the fruit of that unsavory though rightful union—redeemed not only Tamar and her first husband Er. He redeemed also Judah himself, who soon returned to his brothers and became their leader.

The house of Perez has flourished. Boaz, a seventh-generation member of that house, is a wealthy landowner, a noble leader of his community. Instructed and inspired by Ruth's loyal devotion, and grateful for his portion, Boaz has now freely chosen to "repay" toward this outsider the bounty that the outsider Tamar gave to his ancestor Judah: the redemptive gift of a child and heir, who will carry into the next generation the name, the way of life, and the God-seeking hopes and aspirations of his ancestors. And by announcing his intentions in the gates of the city, Boaz inspires the people to give utterance to the deepest meanings of love and marriage and to celebrate the renewing and redemptive power of birth—for individuals, for families, and for the community.

Childbirth

The story lacks only its happy ending. We readers don't have long to wait.

> And Boaz took Ruth, and she became his wife; and he went in unto her, and the Lord gave her conception, and she bore a son. (4:13)

How easy it all turned out to be: marriage, an act of lovemaking, conception, the birth of an heir. Quite the reversal from the start of our story, when, living in the land of Moab and despite ten years of marriage, Ruth had remained childless. Now, in the right land, with the right man, suffused with the right spirit, and accepted into the community, she is barren no more. The Lord blesses her—and this marriage—with a son.

Although many characters in our story speak *about* the Lord, the sentence about His gift of conception to Ruth echoes the only other place where the text reports an action *of* the Lord: namely, His remembrance of the land (1:6). Fertility, whether in relief of famine or removal of barrenness, is a divine gift. Indeed, only with His gift of a child to this special married couple is the Lord's restoration of fruitfulness complete, a completion achieved by re-generative marriage and *chesed* to the stranger. Through this small but emblematic act of renewal, we can anticipate the moral regeneration of the land, so corrupt in the Age of Judges.

We note with more than a little sadness that Ruth, now that she has given birth, will disappear from her story. The name of this exquisite woman will not be mentioned again. Critics of the text will complain that Ruth is in the end reduced to being but a seedbed to her husband and a vessel for the generation of sons. Yet others will see that Ruth has finally been fulfilled: she has at last become a mother in Israel—and of what a lineage! Continuity of the covenant in Israel always requires fathers to circumcise their newborn sons; but they can do so only if the women bear them, and bear them faithfully *within* the covenant. Redemption from death and renewal of life depend on generation, and generation is the province and glory of woman, who embodies and delivers the antidote to mortality.

This is an old story, as old as life itself. At the end of the tale of the Garden of Eden, God teaches the man (*'adam*) that (awareness of) hardship, trouble, and death will permanently be his lot in consequence of his gaining the enlightening but burdensome knowledge of good and bad: "for dust you are and unto dust you shall return" (Genesis 3:19). Astonishingly, however, the man does not despair. A soul-saving passion of hope fixes his mind on the singular piece of good news contained in God's otherwise grim prophecy to the woman: she is going to bear children! His soul uplifted by discovering the redemptive and overflowing powers of woman, the man names her without any reference to himself, as the unique source of life and hope: "and the man called his woman *Chava* (Eve), because she [and only she] was the mother of all living" (Genesis 3:20). On this profound subject, nothing has changed.

The birth of her son may be said to complete Ruth's essential work upon the stage of our story. But giving birth in Ruth's case, unlike in the case of Mother Eve, was the fruit not only of her body but also of her astounding virtue—the offspring of her *chesed*—which she delivered into this disordered community. Knowing these essentials, we have all we need to know about her life.

Following Boaz's speech in the gate, we heard the reaction of the men. Now, after Ruth's delivery of the child, we get the reaction of the women. The men had spoken of both Ruth and Boaz; the women speak mainly about, and only to, Naomi.

> And the women said unto Naomi: "Blessed be
> the Lord, who has not left *you* this day with-
> out a redeemer (*go'el*), and let his name be *famous*
> in Israel. And he shall be to you a *restorer of life*
> (*lemeshiv nefesh*; from *shuv*, "return"), and sustain
> you in old age; for your daughter-in-law (*kallah*),
> who *loves* you, who is *better to you than seven sons*,
> has borne him." (4:14–15; emphasis added)

The women have clearly changed their tune. When Naomi and Ruth returned "empty" from Moab, bereaved and childless, the women gossiped. When Ruth cleaved to Naomi, both of them living on gleanings and forming a world unto themselves, the women were nowhere to be seen. But now, with Ruth's fruitful marriage and Naomi's grandmotherhood—in which they see the hand of God—the women rush forth to celebrate and speak with one voice: their solidarity *as* women is built not on female friendship but on their shared calling of motherhood. One might fault them for their earlier lack of sympathy, but not at all for their current sentiments. The women know in their bones the blessings of which they now speak.

Addressing their remarks to Naomi, and speaking as though the child were hers (rather than Ruth's), the women first praise the Lord for having removed from her the sorrow and stigma of childlessness: He has not withheld from Naomi the redeemer that is her heir. Boaz (along with the Lord) may have been the *agent* of redemption, but the true *go'el*, according to the women, is the newborn son. (Indeed, Boaz, like Ruth, drops out of the narrative with the birth of their son. For the purposes of this story, his work, too, is in the most important sense complete.)[35] And the Lord has allowed not just Ruth but also Naomi to fulfill herself as a mother in Israel. Whereas the men had prayed for Boaz's fame—but merely in Bethlehem—for the newborn son the women pray for fame in all of Israel. They prophesy that the child will restore (*shuv*, "return") Naomi to life—that is, will overcome her despair—and will support her in her old age—that is, will negate her poverty. Finally redeemed, Naomi, too, will have someone to carry forward her line and her life.

In the end, however, the women cannot fail to give credit also to Ruth—even though they will not mention her name. What they say is startling. The new grandson, they imply, will later care for Naomi *because* his mother, Naomi's daughter-in-law, *loves her*. Naomi has given up the female companion of her old age so that her daughter-in-law might be married and raise children of her own. As a reward for such *chesed*, the chorus of women seems to suggest, Naomi will enjoy the loyal devotion of that marriage's offspring—a son born, the text almost says, *of the love* Ruth bears to *Naomi*.

We must not fail to note that, in this tale of love, friendship, marriage, and procreation, the word "love" in the phrase "who loves you"—*'ahevathekh* (from *'ahav*, "love")—occurs only in this one place. The text never speaks of "love" between Ruth and Boaz. Moreover, it never speaks of Naomi's love for Ruth—only of Ruth's (one-sided? unreciprocated?) attachment to Naomi. Yet we should not over-read these absences. The specific term used here is put in the mouth of the women, who may have but a partial or erroneous view of the matter. Besides, as we have already discussed, it would not befit the mutual love of Ruth and Boaz to have them speak about it in public, or to have the text destroy its majesty by naming it. In addition, no serious reader of the book can doubt Naomi's deep love of Ruth, as evidenced by her consistent willingness to elevate Ruth's happiness far above her own. The chorus of women lacks our advantage: they have not read the book.

But the women's most amazing comment is their

claim that her daughter-in-law is *better to Naomi than seven sons*. What does this mean? Are the women right? Would Naomi agree? Would the text? Do we? We offer one suggestion, drawn from the beginning of the Book of Samuel, a book with other suggestive links to the Book of Ruth.[36]

In the very first verses of 1 Samuel, a loving Elkanah tries to comfort his beloved but long-barren and despairing wife Hannah:

> "Hannah, why do you cry? And why do you not eat? And why is your heart grieved? *Am I not better to you than ten sons?*" (1 Samuel 1:8; emphasis added)

Elkanah means well: is not my love and care for you greater than the benefits that might come from mothering a quorum of boys? But his words of consolation are in fact ignorant and insensitive; at best, he completely misunderstands the longings of his wife, just as, years earlier, an ignorant Jacob had similarly failed to appreciate his beloved Rachel's desperate desire for a child (Genesis 30:1–2). The love and devotion of a husband, wonderful though they be, are to a woman no substitute for bringing forth new life, for fulfilling what she alone is natured to do.

Whatever they might have meant by their remark, in one crucial sense the women lauding Naomi and Ruth do not exaggerate: seven sons cannot produce a grandchild; only a daughter or a daughter-in-law can. Ruth, precisely because she has left her mother-in-law for a husband, has assured Naomi's future place in Israel.

The women rejoice with Naomi. Naomi, making no answer, rejoices in the child—and we rejoice for her:

And Naomi took the child, and laid it in her bosom, and became nurse (or "foster-mother"; *'omeneth*, from *'aman*, "to support" or "be faithful") unto it. (4:16)

Awakened from her sorrows, already "returned to life," Naomi embraces the child with the primal maternal gesture as if it were her own, a replacement for the ones she has lost. The language suggests that Naomi adopts the child, symbolically if not literally. Traditional commentators say that Ruth delivered the child, but Naomi raised it as her own.

The neighboring women take a similar view of the matter.

And the women her neighbors gave it a name, saying: "There is a son (*ben*) born to Naomi"; and they called his name Obed (*'oved*; "serving"); he is the father of Jesse, the father of David. (4:17)

Seeing Naomi with a child at her bosom, her neighbors see it as a divine gift. Accordingly, they rush to atone for their previous disdain. Indeed, it is these neighbor women who give the child its name—as if this miracle-baby belongs somehow also to the community.

In naming the child Obed, "serving," the women intuit what is special about him and express their hope for his future. Prophetically, they see that this godsend of a child will serve the God who sent him and the people who carry God's Way. Filling in their thought, the text clarifies the *way* that Obed served: he became the father of Jesse, who became the father of . . . David.

First-time readers of the Book of Ruth are often shocked at this surprise ending. Who would have imagined that our miniature domestic story, centering on the private life of a loyal and gracious woman from a despised nation, would turn out to be, among other things, the backstory to King David? Who would have imagined that the ultimate goal of this simple tale—how an alien woman's *chesed* replicates itself in the lives of Naomi, Boaz, and the men and women of Bethlehem—would culminate in political and poetic greatness?

With the long-awaited birth, and the surprising mention of David, the book of Ruth comes to an end by providing the full genealogy of the great king.

> Now these are the generations of Perez: Perez begot Hezron; and Hezron begot Ram, and Ram begot Amminadab; and Amminadab begot Nahshon, and Nahshon begot Salmon; and Salmon begot Boaz, and Boaz begot Obed; and Obed begot Jesse, and Jesse begot David. (4:18–22)

Not since Genesis, with its full genealogies of Noah and Abraham (Genesis 5 and 11), has anyone—not even Moses—received such a ten-generational account of his ancestry. The founder of this chain is Perez, son of Judah by his Adullamite daughter-in-law Tamar. But the critical link in the chain is the man of the seventh generation, Boaz, whose deeds of *chesed* in our present story redeem not only Naomi and Elimelech, Mahlon and Ruth, and his fellow Bethlehemites. They also redeem, looking backward, his ancestor Judah and, looking forward, the entire people of Israel. Barrenness is no more. Hope is back in the saddle. David, the Lord's anointed, is on his way.

Birth, Redemption, and the Way of Israel

We have completed our commentary on the entire text, working line by line. It remains for us to revisit a few of its larger themes and to offer suggestions about the meaning and importance of the book as a whole.

Unlike most books of the Hebrew Bible, the Book of Ruth, as we have seen, reports no grand political or theological events. No battles are fought. No laws are proclaimed, and no prophecies are delivered. The Lord, though spoken of, does not Himself speak. What we have instead is a modest domestic tale of woe and redemption, opening with famine, emigration, out-marriage, death, and bereavement and ending with return, harvest, in-marriage, birth, and rejoicing. Concerned—uniquely in the biblical canon—with the fate of two women, it is a prosaic story of ordinary life in the Promised Land. Yet precisely for this reason, it is of paradigmatic significance for the People of the Book. The Torah had set forth moral-spiritual principles for a people whose *raison d'être* is to enact the sanctification of everyday life—in the home, on the land, with one's neighbors. The story of Ruth gives us a concrete and glowing model of the redemptive power of those principles in action.

The Children of Israel were long ago summoned at Sinai to a life devoted to righteousness and holiness, to be lived in service to the Lord in the Promised Land. At the center of that life—and at the center of the book of Ruth—are commitments to family continuity and attachments to the land.

It is only through marriage and especially through procreation that the covenantal way of life is transmitted and preserved from generation to generation; should a man die without an heir, his brothers and kin are morally obligated to sire for him a son. And it is only through attachment to its own portion of the Promised Land that every family maintains its place in the holy community; should a man be economically compelled to sell his land, his kinsmen are encouraged to redeem it. Even if no one does, ownership will revert to his family in the next Jubilee year (Leviticus 25: 8ff.), during which all are reminded that the land ultimately belongs to the Lord: "for the land is Mine; for you are strangers (*gerim*) and settlers (*toshavim*) with Me" (Leviticus 25:23).

In a word: in Israel, begetting and belonging are of the essence. Members of the community should not disappear without a trace and land should not be permanently alienated. The community should avoid an enduring division between the landed and the non-landed. Every family should be rooted in the land, able to sustain its life, generation after generation, in service to the Lord.

The way of Israel, something new under the sun, differs sharply from the dominant alternatives of the ancient—and modern—world, especially the ways of the Egyptians and the Canaanites against which God's Way is explicitly defined in the Torah. The Egyptians, obsessed with the affront of mortality, embalm the bodies of their kingly dead and then in pursuit of bodily immortality seek technological means to reanimate them. By contrast, in Israel everyone's mortal remains are given respectful burial, and a forward-looking answer to mortality is given instead in procreation and cultural transmission. The law of forbidden unions (Leviticus 18), the central text of Israel's call to holiness, is directed explicitly against Egyptian and Canaanite practices of incest, sodomy, and bestiality—unrestrained sexual practices that are *in principle* indifferent to generation. This law not only aims to channel sexual energy toward its procreative purpose. It also seeks to keep clear the lines of who belongs to whom, in the service of enhancing parental responsibility for children. In a direct attack on the Canaanite practice of child-sacrifice, the Israelites are forbidden to offer their children to Molech (Leviticus 18:21): a one-sentence child-centered key to the entire chapter about forbidden unions. Most important, the law insists on introducing sacred distance, respect, and reverence into family life, precisely to produce holiness, *qedushah*, in that all-too-intimate nest of humanity that all-too-often becomes instead a den of iniquity and a seedbed of tragedy.

From its very beginning, the preeminent status of marriage and family life (beginning with the Decalogue's "Honor your father and mother") has distinguished the way of Israel from the other prominent strands of Western civilization. For the ancient Greeks, the family was a sub-political institution, war and politics were the fields of glory and honor, and male friendship (including homoerotic love) was more highly regarded than marriage and the love of man for woman. For early Christianity, parochial attachments to one's own kith and kin were regarded as obstacles to the duty of universal love ("Leave your father and mother and follow me" [Matthew 10:34–38]), and priestly celibacy became a cultural ideal.

In keeping with its contrasting preoccupation with

holiness and the sanctification of family life, the Torah's teaching about marriage and procreation is not merely forward-looking and personal. Concerned with perpetuating not just life but a *way* of life, it also looks backward, securely linking the future to the covenantal past and to Sinai. For the same reason, it looks not just linearly but also laterally, serving the larger community as well as the immediate family, primarily by correcting the tragic flaws of the natural family uninstructed.

As we learn from the story of Cain and Abel, brothers are by nature *un*-brotherly. Absent moral instruction, they are adversaries, rivals to the point of fratricide. What they share is only their common origin (the Greek word for brother is *autadelphos*, "same + womb"). Thereafter, their lives become like parallel—or, rather, diverging—lines that have no natural meeting point. Once they leave their family of origin for their family of perpetuation, those two ties and identities will be in tension with each other: devotion to your brother is in principle at odds with devotion to your wife and children.[37] To make matters worse, in societies where nature is made the ground of custom and primogeniture is the rule, no one is his brother's keeper. Because of an accident of birth, younger sons count for naught. (The paradigmatic younger son is Abel, whose name, *Hevel*, is homonymous with a Hebrew word that means "breath-that-vanishes.")

The Torah's prescription of levirate (and levirate-like) marriages directly addresses these problems. Husbands in these marriages serve the interests of brothers (or kinsmen) as well as their own: the first sons "belong" to the deceased, subsequent sons are their own. Brothers become their brothers' keepers. Kinsmen redeem their kinsmen. Everyone's place in the community is secured and the web of communal relations is strengthened. The covenantal community, living toward the future with reverence for the past, flourishes from generation to generation. Redeeming the link in the chain that was severed in Moab, the marriage of Boaz and Ruth makes the point in spades: their union gives rise to David, the poet king whose deeds unite the people and whose immortal psalms, in praise of the Lord, their descendants sing to the present day.

Turning to the Israelites' relation to the land, we see that it also differs from the exploitative ways of Egypt and the submissive ways of Canaan. Land ownership in Egypt was centralized under Pharaoh's control, people were displaced from their own land to work without respite on Pharaoh's building projects, and the earth's produce was hoarded under his control. The Canaanites, for their part, venerated the earth and its fertility and worshiped nature gods and goddesses in earthy rituals of wild abandon. By contrast, in Israel an intimate relationship—neither irreverent mastery nor worshipful submission, but stewardship—is forged between the people and their land, understood to belong not to them but to the Lord.

Israel's special attitude toward the land influences human relations within the community. Open-handed generosity, not acquisitive hoarding, is the celebrated cultural ideal, in gratitude for the Lord's bountiful gifts. The corners of the field and all fallen grain are donated for gleaning by the poor. The land itself is given sabbatical rest every seventh year, and its spontaneous produce is again left for the poor, for widows and orphans, and for the stranger. That Boaz meets Ruth in the field where she is gleaning inspires Boaz to act as an Israelite and not just as the owner of his land.

In another of its unique features, the Torah that defines the Israelites through its constitutive laws contains a nuanced yet humane teaching about strangers. On the one hand, Israel is to avoid—indeed, to abhor—certain practices of the neighboring pagans, beginning with idolatry and slavery and ending in immorality and iniquity. On the other hand, any individual stranger who dwells among the Israelites must be treated as an equal before the law and must be respected as a fellow human being, equally a creature in the image of God. Holding these two notions together in practice is often a challenge, and never more so than when the stranger hails from an enemy nation. Our story gives us a concrete and edifying example of how to meet—and surmount—that challenge.

The Book of Ruth repeatedly makes much of the fact that its title character is an outsider, an outsider who gradually becomes an insider: Ruth is a foreign woman who becomes the wife, and shortly the widow, of a sojourning Israelite man; she then chooses to move (with Naomi) to the Land of Israel, presumably adopting Israelite ways; and she eventually marries a prominent man—indeed, a "legislating" man—of the Israelite community. Commentators, traditional and modern, see in this story a corrective to Israelite chauvinism and ill treatment of foreigners.

Today, some people use this story not only to combat xenophobia, but also to promote full *acceptance* of the "Other"—even, in some cases, to celebrate out-marriage with strangers. That Ruth is a Moabite—hailing from a most abhorred nation, deserving permanent exclusion from Israel—clinches, they believe, their interpretation: if this epitome of "otherness" can merit acceptance and inclusion, so should any outsider.

This reading is at best partial. Ruth does not represent some abstract and generalized "Other." She remains, almost to the end of the story, very specifically a Moabitess. Nothing in the story casts doubt on the Bible's wholesale rejection of the ways of Moab or encourages multicultural celebrations and exchanges: the failure of Elimelech's move to Moab, his death and the death of his sons after taking Moabite wives, and the barrenness of those marriages all fit the view that the ways of Moab are deadly to the way of Israel and should be rejected absolutely. If Ruth becomes a celebrated heroine in Israel, it must be *despite* her otherness. It must have everything to do with her singular virtue and superior character.

As we have seen, Ruth is a woman of valor and an angel of *chesed*. She is unswervingly loyal and devoted to her mother-in-law Naomi, in response to her neediness and goodness. For Naomi's sake (and for her dead husband's), she willingly abandons her own Moabite home, family, and gods, and freely moves to a strange land, with different ways and a demanding God. As Boaz says, she practices *chesed* to both the living and the dead. She humbles herself to glean in the fields for Naomi's sake, and in doing so inspires Boaz to practice *chesed* toward her. Later told by Naomi to, in effect, play Lot's daughter with Boaz, she acts chastely and resolutely. The *chesed* she shows Boaz on the threshing floor is again reciprocated: he refuses to treat her as his ancestor Judah treated Tamar, but rises instead to redeem her—and her dead husband—in marriage.

Ruth's *chesed* sustains Naomi, inspires Boaz to be his kinsman's keeper, and finally enables the entire community to practice hospitality to the stranger who has cast her virtuous lot with them. Through Ruth's doing (and Boaz's), the community is rescued from its lapsed practices and iniquitous ways. Lawful marriage is reaffirmed as the communal ideal. The community is reunited around the redemptive gift of childbirth. The way is paved for proper sovereignty through the anticipated arrival of a God-fearing king. In a word, Ruth's *chesed* enables the Israelites to return and live up to their calling.

These extraordinary *national* effects of Ruth's virtue oblige us to revise our earlier judgment that her "strangeness" is irrelevant to her heroism or to the story's teaching about "the other." In the corrupt time of "the judging of the judges," Israel has to be reminded of its national calling precisely by an outsider—indeed, by a member of an enemy people. Fortunately, although summoned to cultivate *chesed*—a human embodiment of divine grace—Israel has no monopoly on it. Its redemptive virtue can crop up anywhere, even in evil regimes and decadent cultures. Israel renews and does honor to itself, to *chesed*, and to God—as it does here under Boaz's singular leadership—whenever it recognizes, and offers a true home for ("spreads it wing over"), such remarkable devotion. Ruth's "otherness" is therefore a central aspect of our story's teaching and of its own remarkable grace.[38]

This thought reminds us that there is an additional

group of characters who gain from the story a more general lesson about strangers: that group is ourselves, its readers. Over and over, we are reminded of Ruth's Moabite origins and identity, not so much because the text sees Ruth mainly in that light, but because *we* do. Mirroring and feeding our own tendency to treat her national origin as destiny, even while we see increasing evidence of her Israelite spirit, we are shocked into a proper inward appreciation of Ruth only when Boaz wipes away her origins by making her his wife. In this tale of redemption, we readers are not excluded.

Two loose ends need tying up. First, how can we square our story's celebration of marriage and procreation with the incestuous origins of its major characters? The way of Israel, as we have emphasized, is characterized by—one may almost say *founded* upon—an implacable opposition to sexual iniquity and especially to incest. Yet here we celebrate a marriage—and one leading to Israel's greatest king!—whose roots are doubly polluted: Ruth, a direct descendant of Lot and his daughter; Boaz, a direct descendant of Judah and his daughter-in-law. Several suggestions appeal to us.

First, those tainted unions happened long ago and before the Torah that condemns them was given at Sinai. One may even say that the Torah's teachings were specifically directed against those very deeds in Israel's (and humankind's) uninstructed origins.

Second, there were mitigating circumstances in those ancient iniquities. In both cases, the women—Lot's daughter and Tamar, neither of them an Israelite—were seeking offspring, not mere self-gratification: the for-

mer, to people the earth after the holocaust of Sodom
and Gomorrah, the latter, to raise a son to her dead
husband. They were partisans of new life, not seek-
ers of selfish pleasure (as was Judah with Tamar)—reasons, perhaps, why they and their iniquitous deeds were
not condemned in the text. Their natalist inclinations,
once brought under God's gracious covenant with Israel,
serve perpetuation not only of life but also of an elevated
way of life, aspiring to righteousness and holiness.

Third, the way of Israel allows for second chances.
Natural origins and bloodline identity are not destiny.
Repentance, reform, and the embrace of righteousness
and holiness are open to everyone.

Finally, according to the Torah, the iniquities of the
fathers will be visited upon the children, but only to
the third or fourth generation; pollution persists in the
world, but not indefinitely. By contrast, God's grace, we
are told, will be bestowed unto the thousandth generation upon those who keep His commandments (Exodus 20:5–6). In the present case, the Lord bestows His
own *chesed* upon those exemplars of virtue and *chesed*,
Ruth and Boaz. Thanks to their adherence to the ways
of *chesed*, the Lord redeems the stains of ancient iniquity, and the abominations of incests past are transfig-
ured into the line of King David. History is not destiny;
redemption is possible, even after the worst of sins.

We close with another look at the title of the book.
Ruth is without doubt one of literature's loveliest crea-
tures. It is, as we have stressed, her deeds of *chesed* that
turn the world around—for Naomi, for Boaz, for the
community, and for the Jewish people. At critical times,

she takes the initiative—to go back with Naomi, to go gleaning in the fields, to instruct Boaz at the threshing floor. She speaks up for herself and for those near and dear. For all these reasons, *chesed* begetting *chesed*, the Lord rains grace upon her, in the form of marriage and motherhood. She deserves her immortal fame.

Yet, off to the side and never in the limelight, the marriage and motherhood of Ruth have another author, her mother-in-law Naomi. These blessings are the preoccupation of Naomi from the start. Ruth, the Moabite, comes down eloquently for female friendship; Naomi, speaking for the way of Israel, holds out for marriage and procreation: Naomi will not rest until Ruth lies in the bed of her husband. Although the odds are slim, she never loses hope for her widowed daughter-in-law. She refuses to dwell on her own miseries but keeps her eyes and ears open on Ruth's behalf. From behind the scenes, she waits patiently and prudently for the right opportunity, not spoiling Ruth's chances by haste or wishful thinking. And when the occasion finally arrives, Naomi springs quickly into action, coaching Ruth toward a most propitious—and redemptive—match. When the marriage proves fruitful, Naomi celebrates the birth as if it were her own; and the entire community celebrates with her—and Ruth is moved to the side. In all these ways, Naomi faithfully serves as God's partner in upholding and perpetuating His Torah's chosen way. Her "principles"—marriage and children—are vindicated in the end.

So why, then, is the book not named for Naomi? And why, if it is properly named for Ruth, does the epilogue end by celebrating Naomi? The question troubled the refined literary sensibilities of Maurice Samuel, who partly on these grounds thought that the book should have been called the Book of Naomi. In his lovely essay on Naomi, he offers a whimsical explanation:

> I have the feeling that the recorder originally thought of Ruth, the more obviously dramatic of the two women, as the heroine, and that is how he tried to write it; and certainly Ruth is one of the loveliest and most moving beings known to us; and it is not a question of comparing her with Naomi but of finding out with what closing impression the recorder wanted to leave us. I feel sure that he chose Ruth and her fate as focus and climax before he began the writing; but as he went along, Naomi, with whom the story opens, drew him more and more, even as she had drawn her daughters-in-law, and he was not quite aware of it, and by the time he ended he had forgotten what he started out to say.[39]

We have a different suggestion. The book is named for Ruth because the loving and self-effacing Naomi would not have had it any other way.

Authors' Afterthoughts

Hannah This entire project—from studying the text to writing this book—is a testament to my beloved Gaga's spirit and life's work. She taught great texts in a wisdom-seeking manner, bringing the texts to life by encouraging her students to ponder their hard questions and to make them their own. Although I was never privileged to attend her classes, it seemed so natural to begin reading Ruth, a text she loved, in her wisdom-seeking way. It was as if she were smiling down on us, helping us fill the void left by her passing with the same questions, thoughts, and friendly conversations that would have graced her classroom—questions about love and friendship, questions about familial and communal obligation. Even the special bond formed between my Zaydeh and me through this process was the work of Gaga's smiling hand, working Naomi-like behind the scenes. Although Gaga cannot see the fruit of our efforts, it could not have happened without her. For her example and guidance, I am eternally grateful.

Leon Apart from two writing projects that I shared with my wife Amy, no intellectual or professional activ-

ity in my long life has been as meaningful and reward-
ing as this one. Reading Ruth with Hannah, begun in
grief, was from start to finish a life-affirming weaving
together of the personal and the intellectual, of the philosophical and the familial. In the company of fresh eyes
and an eager heart, a lost insight of Amy's was recovered, revivified, and perpetuated into the next generation. The self-conscious experience of reading with my
granddaughter this magnificent story of intergenera-
tional continuity and remembrance of the dead, and
the subsequent experiences of recording, reconsidering,
and rewriting our interpretative commentary, have con-
firmed for me the redemptive powers of faithful devotion, new birth, and cultural transmission. In keeping
with the spirit and teaching of the book, my loss of Amy
has been partly redeemed also by Hannah's Ruth-like
(and Amy-like) *chesed*—her gracious kindness and loving devotion—which she has steadily showered on me
and on Amy's memory. I am overwhelmed with gratitude for these blessings.

Acknowledgments

The authors are indebted to Paul Dry for welcoming us onto his list. We are grateful for his enthusiasm and encouragement, his wise editorial judgment, and his gracious manner. Working with Paul has been a pleasure from beginning to end.

We are grateful also to Eric Cohen and Neal Kozodoy of the Tikvah Fund for their multifaceted support. An early reader and keen promoter of the manuscript, Eric arranged with Paul Dry Books to produce a special Tikvah imprint of the book. Our friend Neal kindly contributed his superb editorial talents, tightening the text and improving the prose on nearly every page. Antón Barba-Kay, Naomi Brodsky, Harvey Flaumenhaft, Rabbi Shmuel Herzfeld, Robbie Krauthammer, Alan Rubenstein, and Suzanne Singer read the entire text in draft, offering encouragement and useful suggestions; several lengthy conversations with Alan produced new insights that we incorporated into the Notes. Robbie and Suzanne were also helpful consultants in finding art for the cover.

Last, but really first, our beloved Amy Kass of blessed memory has been from the start our inspiration. We have read, conversed, and written guided by her spirit. We dedicate this book to her memory.

Notes

1. For a fuller exploration of this rich story (which occupies the whole of Genesis 38), see Chapter 17 of Leon R. Kass, *The Beginning of Wisdom: Reading Genesis* (Free Press, 2003), especially the section entitled "The Other Candidate: The Education of Judah."

2. Here is another echo of the story of Judah and Tamar but with Naomi in the place of Judah: Judah also lost two sons, whose deaths similarly left a widow childless.

3. In the prologue to our story, the actions all belong to the men: "Elimelech went . . . to sojourn"; the sons "took them wives . . . they dwelt there . . . they died, both of them." This one "action" of Naomi is passive: she was "left behind." (Our thanks to Alan Rubenstein for this observation.)

4. The linkage between the two kinds of fertility—crops and children—and God's providence in securing them both will later become explicit. The *only* other deed in the entire book that is directly attributed to the Lord is Ruth's pregnancy (4:13).

5. The conflation of "bride" and "daughter-in-law" can be extremely problematic, when the *father*-in-law is involved. Three of the four uses of *kallah* in Genesis refer to Tamar, Judah's daughter-in-law by whom he has children.

And the only other two uses of *kallah* in the Torah occur in Leviticus, to prohibit in the strongest possible terms all sexual relations between a man and his daughter-in-law (Leviticus 18:15; 20:12). What Judah did in ignorance and what Tamar did in desperate cunning becomes a capital offense for both the man and his *kallah*. And yet, as already noted, a descendant of that union of Judah and Tamar plays a heroic role in our present tale. We return to this matter at the end.

6. The Midrashic commentary on the Book of Ruth offers a darker interpretation. After pointing out that the usual name of the family home (and of the family itself) is *beth 'av*, "the father's house," the Midrash suggests that one read *beth 'immah*, "her mother's house," as *beth 'umathah*, "her ethnic [or her people's] home." R. Meir comments that, among the Moabites (and other Gentiles) "women cannot assume to know the identity of their fathers, since their women are promiscuous. For this reason, Gentiles identify with their mothers and their mother's families. That accounts for . . . Naomi's request that her daughters-in-law return to their mothers' homes. *Beth 'immah* does indeed become *beth 'umathah*, her ethnic home." (*The Midrash Rabbah: Ruth*, Feldheim, 2003, pp. 95–96.)

7. As testimony for Naomi's thesis, one cannot help being reminded of Tolstoy's wonderfully vivid before-and-after portrait in *War and Peace* of the transformation in the lively and impetuous young Countess Natásha Rostova upon becoming a mother.

> Natásha had married in the early spring of 1813, and in 1820 already had three daughters besides a son for whom she had longed and whom she was now nursing. She had grown stouter and broader, so that it was difficult to recognize in this robust, motherly woman the slim, lively Natásha of former days. Her features were more defined and had a calm, soft, and serene expres-

sion. . . . The old fire very rarely kindled in her face now. That happened only when, as was the case that day, her husband returned home, or a sick child was convalescent, . . . or on the rare occasions when some-thing happened to induce her to sing, a practice she had quite abandoned since her marriage. At the rare moments when the old fire did kindle in her handsome, fully developed body she was even more attractive than in former days.

. . . All who had known Natásha before her marriage wondered at the change in her as at something extraor-dinary. *Only the old countess with her maternal instinct had realized that all Natásha's outbursts had been due to her need of children and a husband . . . and her mother was now surprised at the surprise expressed by those who had never understood Natásha, and she kept saying that she had always known that Natásha would make an exem-plary wife and mother.* (Louise and Aylmer Maude trans-lation, Norton, 1966, pp. 1281–82; emphasis added.)

8. The truth of this teaching—that *chesed* ("grace" or "loyal devotion") is reciprocated—is represented in classical antiquity by the image of the three Graces dancing in a cir-cle, hand in hand (perhaps most famously depicted in art by Sandro Botticelli's *La Primavera*). The Roman philosopher Seneca explains the image:

What is the meaning of this dance of sisters in a circle, hand in hand? It means that the course of a benefit is from hand to hand, back to the giver; that the beauty of the whole chain is lost if a single link fails, and that it is fairest when it proceeds in unbroken regular order. . . . Their faces are cheerful, as those human beings who give or receive benefits are wont to be. They are young, because the memory of benefits ought not to grow old.

(From *De Beneficiis*; quoted in Amy A. Kass, ed., *Giving Well, Doing Good*, Indiana University Press, 2008, p. v.)

9. Maurice Samuel (1895–1972) was a Romanian-born British and American Jewish thinker, writer, and translator. His beautiful appreciation of Naomi captures exquisitely her mood and attitude:

> For their sakes she would leave them, lest they should continue to be involved in her unhappy destiny. It cannot be denied that Naomi's mood was one of despair. She had lost faith in life—in her own life, that is; she was not to be granted that which could make her happy—namely, *the sight of the happiness of those she loved*. It was best, then, for her to remove herself from them; *they might yet find happiness if she did not seek to share it*. And so by the roadside she tried to take *an everlasting farewell of these beloved links with the beloved dead*. ("An Idyl of Old Age" in *Certain People of the Book*. Knopf, 1955, p. 106; emphasis added.)

10. For an outstanding discussion of Orpah, see the essay "Ruth" by Cynthia Ozick, in her collection, *Metaphor and Memory* (Knopf, 1989), pp. 240–264.

11. See Deuteronomy 10:20, 11:22, 13:5, and 30:20.

12. Dr. Leonard Groopman has suggested to us that Ruth's passion for Naomi is akin to the phenomenon known in psychoanalysis as "transference," in which Ruth has (unconsciously) shifted to Naomi, as substitute, the passionate attachment she had to her late husband. We ourselves regard Ruth's cleaving to Naomi as a manifestation not of her grief or psychic distress but rather of her great virtue and capacity for love. Her subsequent behavior bears this out.

13. Samuel, *Certain People of the Book*, p. 108. We will later learn that Elimelech had owned a small plot of land,

which he had either sold before leaving for Moab or which was in possession of squatters who had seized it after he had gone. Destitute and powerless, the returned Naomi is unable to rectify the situation: she can neither redeem it from its current owner nor reclaim it from squatters. According to the law regarding redemption of land, one of Naomi's kinsmen should have bought from her the right to redeem the land for the family; but neither Boaz nor the unnamed kinsman had as yet seen fit to do so.

14. We are indebted to Sarah Kass for showing us the special significance of gleaning and for suggesting some of the central ideas in this paragraph and the next.

15. The primary formulation is given in the so-called Holiness Code of Leviticus:

> And when you reap the harvest of your land, you shall not wholly reap the corner of your field, neither shall you gather the gleaning of your harvest. And you shall not glean your vineyard, neither shall you gather the fallen fruit of your vineyard; you shall leave them for the poor and for the stranger: I am the Lord your God. (Leviticus 19:9–10)

The other relevant passages are Leviticus 23:22 and Deuteronomy 24:19–21.

16. Traditional commentators credit Boaz with originating the use of this noble and pious expression—"the Lord be with you"—as a common form of greeting.

17. See Deuteronomy 8:17–18. We thank Judah Mandelbaum for this reference and for the main ideas of this paragraph.

18. Says one traditional commentator, trying to fill the descriptive void: "she would never inelegantly stoop to take the gleanings, but would gather them either standing or squatting." We prefer to think that, not just here but through-

out, the text preserves silence about Ruth's appearance so that
we learn to see her inner beauty—which, as in many such
cases, can also mysteriously reveal itself on the surface but
not in easily describable terms.

19. Another possibility, suggested to us by Alan Rubenstein and based on a translation of the verb *ta'amod* as "she
stood" or "she remained": Ruth has been standing still since
she arrived at Boaz's part of the field, waiting for permission to glean—which the prejudiced overseer has refused to
give her. This reading could also explain why Boaz first no-
ticed her: a motionless woman standing to the side as the
other maidens gleaned; and it would also enable us to read
Boaz's next speech as finally giving her permission to glean
in his fields. Despite these attractive possibilities, we stick
to our reading: in fact, we have already been told that Ruth
"gleaned in the field after the reapers" (2:3) and, as the overseer himself observes, she has continued to do so tirelessly.

20. Some sources suggest that the two words in fact
have a common *n-k-r* root; others insist that the roots are
distinct. Whether or not they are indeed related, Ruth's
question about recognition and foreignness puts the critical
issue squarely before Boaz—and also before the surround-
ing reapers and us, the readers.

21. About Boaz's phrase, "It was indeed told me," Alan
Rubenstein astutely observes that in fact "we've been given
no reason to think that this recognition of Ruth's greatness
is shared by others. The other Bethlehemites, after all, seem
content to have left Naomi and Ruth in their state of desti-
tution and misery. In claiming to speak for other putative
admirers of Ruth, what he [Boaz] is doing—and he does
it repeatedly—is legislating. Others will think what he asserts they think because he is that kind of man wielding that
kind of authority: an *'ish gibor chayil*." ("Beyond Sighing
and Swooning: Love in the Hebrew Bible," *Mosaic*. January

12, 2017; https://mosaicmagazine.com/observation/2017/01/
beyond-sighing-and-swooning-love-in-the-hebrew-bible/)

22. Yael Ziegler offers a beautiful exploration of Boaz's
"poetry" in her splendid commentary, *Ruth: From Alienation
to Monarchy* (Maggid Books, 2015), a work we encountered
only at the end of our studies.

23. Some Jewish mystics have offered a different account
of this idea:

> The Kabbalists explain that when a woman marries,
> her husband's spirit enters her body, where it remains
> even after his death, until it is replaced by the spirit of
> another husband. All this time, it stirs within her and
> gives her no rest. This was Naomi's intention in seek-
> ing "a rest" for Ruth, that "it may be well" with her.
> Although it would not be well for Mahlon, whose spirit
> would be expelled, Naomi's primary concern was for
> Ruth (Moshe Alshich [1508–1593], *Iggereth Sh'muel*).
> (Quoted in *The Five Megilloth*, ed. Rev. Dr. Abraham
> Cohen, Soncino Press, 1984, p. 129)

At first glance, this notion seems at odds with the suggestion
that the dead husband (Mahlon) will be redeemed through
his wife's remarriage and childbirth. But it actually fits very
nicely. His spirit can find rest only when a redeemer begets
a son who will be his (Mahlon's) heir, securing his future
against full extinction.

An additional suggestion with respect to the Hebrew
noun for "rest": Naomi's change of the word's gender from
the feminine *menuchah* to the masculine *manoach* also implies that she, too, can find rest via the redemption that
may come through a husband for Ruth: Naomi will have a
(grand)son in place of Mahlon.

24. This is the evidence cited by Rashi to support his
comment that in dressing only after she had reached the

threshing floor, Ruth avoided calling unwanted and disreputable attention to herself.

25. Three times in Exodus it denotes the "enchantments"—the *secret* arts—of Pharaoh's magicians, as they try to match the first three plagues produced by Moses—blood, frogs, and lice (Exodus 7:22; 8:3; 8:14). The other two uses occur in the vexed relations between King Saul and David: once when Saul has his servants *secretly* flatter David into accepting his daughter Michal as a wife, to make him more vulnerable to attack by the Philistines; once when David comes upon the sleeping Saul, now overtly his enemy, and *secretly* cuts off the skirt of his robe to let Saul know that he could have killed him (1 Samuel 18:22, 24:4)

26. The Hebrew word *'amathekha*, "your maidservant," used in the Book of Ruth only in this sentence as a gesture of humility, would also, if written without the vowel pointings, look identical to *'emethekha*, that is, "your truth." Readers seeing the one are invited to think the other.

27. Alan Rubenstein, personal communication.

28. *'Esheth chayil*, "a woman of valor," are the opening words of (and, hence, the name for) the splendid paean of praise from the Book of Proverbs (31:10–31) that is traditionally recited on Sabbath eve in Jewish homes to honor the woman of the house.

29. The Midrash, not surprisingly, clearly favors the last, but with an edifying qualification:

> R. Berechiah added, "God did not arrange this miraculous timing just to alleviate Boaz's anxiety. There was another reason as well. . . . [Quoting R. Eliezer:] '**Boaz did his part** by overcoming his evil inclination and promising to act promptly on her behalf. **Ruth did her part** by heeding Naomi and going to the threshing floor at night. She risked her safety and also rejection by Boaz for approaching him in this manner. **Naomi did**

her part by urging Ruth to get married, even though it meant that she would be living alone from then on. In light of all these noble actions, **the Holy Blessed One said,** "Now **I too will do My part** to expedite the process."'" When someone performs a good deed with particular fervor and enthusiasm, God helps him complete the task rapidly and completely. This explains why God arranged for the redeemer's fortuitous arrival. (*The Midrash Rabbah: Ruth, op. cit.,* p. 229; emphasis in original.)

30. The usual translation of this sentence, accommodating English syntax, begins with the subject of the verb: "Naomi, that is come back out of the field of Moab, sells the parcel of land, which was our brother Elimelech's." But Boaz's rhetorical purpose requires that he begin with the land and only then mention Naomi. Note also the presence of the verb "to return," *shuv,* its penultimate appearance in the book (see 4:15, and below).

31. Lest we suspect that Boaz is also inventing the *existence* of land in Naomi's possession and available for sale, we remind ourselves that each family is entitled to its own portion of the Promised Land, even should the owners be forced to alienate it temporarily.

The status of the land in question, however, is genuinely puzzling. If Naomi still owns the land that was her husband's, why would she need to live off Ruth's gleanings? Also, the verb "to sell," *makhar,* is in the perfective form, implying that the sale has already been completed: but when and to whom might she or Elimelech have sold it? Two alternative situations seem most plausible. (1) Elimelech sold the land before leaving for Moab. Naomi, now destitute, cannot redeem it herself; but she can transfer ("sell") the obligation-right of redemption, which will go either to *peloni 'almoni* or—as both he and Naomi hope—to Boaz. (2) Alterna-

tively, the land had never been sold, squatters took possession of it during Naomi's absence in Moab, and *now* an
outside benefactor is needed to redeem the land and to keep
it in the family. Naomi has already *determined* to sell the
land—hence, the perfect form of the verb.

32. For a discussion of the linkage of the two commandments, see Yossi Prager, "*Megillat Ruth*: A Unique
Story of *Torat Hesed*," *Tradition*, Vol. 35, No. 4 (Winter
2001), pp. 15–22. Boaz does not deserve all the credit
for this insight. We could say that he got it the night
before from Ruth, and we could also say that Ruth got it
from Naomi, who, behind the scenes, directs the plot.

33. The argument that this is not at all a love story is
best made by Yael Ziegler in her *Ruth: From Alienation to
Monarchy*, cited above. Alan Rubenstein's essay "Beyond
Sighing and Swooning," quoted earlier and soon again, was
written in response to Ziegler.

34. In "Beyond Sighing and Swooning," Rubenstein
carefully and persuasively collects in one place the evidence
for this conclusion; all of it is already present, albeit scat-
tered, in our account.

35. In line with this idea, there is a Midrash—*Ruth
Zuta*, 4:13—that says the Boaz died on his wedding night,
after having consummated the marriage and sown his seed.

36. The events reported there occur not very long after
the time of the events presented in the Book of Ruth. The
latter take place late in the period of judges and the book
concludes with the birth (just announced) of the grand-
father of David, Israel's second king. The book of Samuel
begins with the (soon to be announced) birth—to Hannah—of the prophet Samuel, who will anoint Saul as Israel's
first king. The literary link may not be accidental. Tradition
credits Samuel with authorship of both these books. Both
Ruth and Hannah play indispensable roles in the arrival of

the monarchy—and in ending the troubles of the Age of Judges.

37. The classic exposition of this problem is given in Aeschylus' *Oresteia* (and in the *Iliad*). Agamemnon leads the Greeks against Troy to recover Helen for his brother Menelaus. But before he is able to sail, the gods demand that he sacrifice his daughter Iphigenia, a deed that shows him the deep meaning of putting the honor of your brother ahead of the lives of your wife and children. (The sacrifice also pointedly teaches Agamemnon about the loss of innocent life that he is about to cause.) Although victorious in the Trojan War, Agamemnon is murdered on his return by his wife, Clytemnestra. For ten years she has been waiting to avenge his killing of their daughter.

38. We are grateful to Antón Barba-Kay for the main idea of this paragraph.

39. Samuel, *Certain People of the Book, op. cit.*, pp. 126–127.